TO CAROL

My most honest and loving critic,
who pushes me to excellence by her encouragement
and draws me to it by her example.

PREACHING WITH FRESHNESS

Bruce Mawhinney

kregel
PUBLICATIONS

Grand Rapids, MI 49501

Preaching with Freshness

Copyright © 1997 by Bruce Mawhinney

Published by Kregel Publications, a division of Kregel, Inc., P.O. Box 2607, Grand Rapids, MI 49501. Kregel Publications provides trusted, biblical publications for Christian growth and service. Your comments and suggestions are valued.

Cover design: Alan G. Hartman

Library of Congress Cataloging-in-Publication Data
Mawhinney, Bruce.
  Preaching with freshness / Bruce Mawhinney.
     p. cm.
  Originally published: Eugene, Oreg.: Harvest House Publishers, 1991.
    1. Preaching—United States. 2. Christian literature, American. 3. Clergy—United States—Appointment, call, and election. I. Title.
BV4211.2.M29   1997   251—dc21   96-52007
                                                CIP

ISBN 0-8254-3198-0

Acknowledgments

Special thanks go to the following men who allowed me to conduct interviews with them about their insights into great preaching: Dr. James Boice, Dr. D. James Kennedy, Dr. Joel Nederhood, Rev. Kennedy Smartt, Dr. R. C. Sproul, and Dr. John White of Geneva College.

I am especially indebted to Dr. John Gertsner who is now with our Lord. To be both his student and one of the many younger "Timothys" in his life is a precious treasure lavished on me by our gracious Lord. His life, ministry, and preaching has truly adorned the Gospel of God and been the source of immeasurable encouragement and conviction to me.

I want to thank all my friends and colleagues in the Reformed Fellowship Group who responded so kindly and favorably to my early findings.

I also want to thank Dr. Jay Adams for his great encouragement and counsel throughout this project, for his editing advice concerning the actual writing of this book, and for his willingness to be available whenever I needed his help.

Thanks to my dear brothers and sisters in Christ, the people of New Hope Presbyterian Church in Monroeville, Pennsylvania, who had enough vision and generosity to allow me to pursue this project and to use them as my weekly sermon guinea pigs!

Of course, no effort taking such time, expense, and energy could be accomplished without the patient support of family. My special love and thanks to Carol, Paul, and Susan!

Contents

Foreword

What a pleasure to write a foreword to Dr. Bruce Mawhinney's book, *Preaching With Freshness!* I have frequently been asked to do such a thing by other students in the doctoral program at WTS, and sometimes I did so with some reluctance. Not this time! I can wholeheartedly recommend the book you are holding in your hands.

When Pastor Mawhinney determined to write about freshness in preaching, I warned him that the subject he had chosen would require him to do so in a fresh way. At the time I made that remark I had no idea how he would fulfill that assignment; I just knew it would be difficult. But he has more than satisfied my expectations. Not only has he provided adequate insight into what makes preaching fresh, but he has done so in the form of a captivating novel. What a pleasant way to learn!

A novel about preaching—that itself is novel. Before I say another thing, let me quickly tell you that *even if you're not a preacher, and even if you don't care to learn anything about preaching, you're going to enjoy this story!* For the story line alone, you ought to buy the book.

For the first piece of published writing that Bruce has done, this book is a remarkable success. I can only hope that, having developed his gifts as a writer of novels, he will continue to bless the Christian world by addressing other difficult subjects in this form. Wouldn't it be interesting to hear of additional exploits of Pastor Andrews as he tackles New Age teaching creeping into his congregation, as he grapples with complex counseling problems, or even perhaps—as he outdoes Chesterton's Father Brown in solving some mystery?

Perhaps writers of forewords enjoy the prerogative of being as forward as possible in what they say. Everyone knows that they are praising someone else's work, and so at times they go overboard. Yet I don't think I have done so in lauding the efforts of Dr. Bruce Mawhinney. You will pick up this unique book and soon find that you cannot put it down. You'll find yourself reading all the way to its moving, heartwarming climax (no, don't spoil it for yourself by reading ahead!).

Jay E. Adams
Enoree, S.C., 1990

Preface

This book is primarily a book on preaching written to and for preachers. But an interesting phenomenon happened as various laypersons reviewed the manuscript for me with an eye toward such matters as proofreading and clarity of thought. One by one these people responded with enthusiasm to the content of the book, sharing with me how they intended to use and apply various principles from it. In my focus on preachers, I had overlooked a variety of applications which the book has for other people involved in the work of the church.

Some immediately began to apply the preaching principles to their own teaching ministries—Sunday school classes, adult Bible studies, lay preaching, even children's sermons! Church Board leaders (we call them ruling elders in our denomination) saw this as an effective tool for better understanding the calling of their pastors and their own roles in working with their pastors in that high calling.

Finally, there were those who simply reacted with enthusiasm to the narrative itself—to its message of hope and inspiration. One Christian woman said, "This is a story every Christian should read, not just pastors and teachers!"

In writing a book on how to find freshness and new life for preachers and their preaching, my desire was twofold: to be true to the Word of God, and to offer practical advice in the process.

Every principle set forth in the following pages is supported by biblical precedent. My examination of the Word of God was done to see not so much *what* truths the Bible teaches but *how* the Bible teaches truth. In particular, what principles did the Holy Spirit inspire the prophets and apostles to use when they preached? What principles did the Master Preacher, the Word Himself, use?

By studying the Bible to see *how* it says *what* it says, the preacher gains an added dimension of authority in preaching the Word. Not only is the sermon's content based on God's Word, but the methods and principles used to advance that content are also based on the Word of God.

By choosing a narrative rather than a textbook approach, another added dimension is given to the book. Instead of communicating from the classroom, the narrative takes place out in the trenches of the pastorate itself. What good is a set of principles on fresh preaching if they cannot be used realistically by the average preacher?

While this story is fictional, it is also real. The principles scattered throughout the narrative are principles that I have tried and tested in my own ministry, with significant positive effect. I can honestly add, with sudden, dramatic effect! Other pastors also cooperated with me in testing out these ideas before I committed them to writing for publication.

As with any new instrument or tool, some of the principles may seem awkward upon first use. The preacher might even experience a temporary decline in effectiveness until certain new techniques become more familiar. Don't give up after one attempt, but try each one several times until you really feel at home with it.

Finally, in an effort to give busy preachers and teachers of the Word an easy reference tool to go back to again and again, I have included a section written as a seminar on fresh preaching. It gathers together and outlines the key ideas scattered throughout the story.

May God bless you as richly as He has blessed me through these truths!

Bruce Mawhinney

1

The Board Meeting

At midnight Paul Andrews pulled into his driveway. Quietly he entered the house and tiptoed toward the stairway. Susan and the children had long been asleep, so he navigated the familiar route in the dark.

From the hallway above came the sleepy thumping of his beagle's tail as it pounded the floor in friendly welcome. She kept guard each night in her sentinel position on the landing outside the bedroom doors.

At the top of the stairs, Paul bent down and patted her head. By now his eyes had adjusted to the dark hallway. He was able to see his dog, with its black-and-white beagle markings, curled up on her cozy plaid blanket.

"If only you could be a member of our Church Board, Snooper," Paul whispered. "Then I would at least have one vote on my side."

Snooper's tail thumped again at the sound of her master's kind voice.

He carefully stepped over her to get to his bedroom, but first he stopped to peek in on his two sons fast asleep in their bunk beds. After setting the alarm for 5:15 A.M. on his nightstand, he quietly climbed in between the sheets.

"How did it go tonight?" Susan whispered.

"Oh, you startled me," Paul jumped. "I thought you were sound asleep."

"No, just drifting in and out. It was a pretty bad one tonight, wasn't it, Paul?"

"'Pretty bad' isn't the term for it. 'Disastrous' might be better!"

"What happened?" Susan asked, suddenly wide awake. She propped herself up with her pillow and brushed her brown hair away from her eyes. She looked at Paul with anxious anticipation.

"I don't feel much like talking about it. I have a breakfast appointment at 6:15 with Glenn."

"Paul, did it involve you personally?" She pressed.

"I've been a minister for ten years, but I feel more uncertain about myself now than ever before. You'd think I'd have this preaching job figured out by now."

Paul gripped the sides of his head with both hands. The dull pain had begun sometime early that evening, and its pounding grew stronger as the long board meeting had progressed. Now that he was lying down it was thundering as the blood rushed to his head.

"What do you mean, honey?" Her voice was assuring. She had no intention of extending the confrontation he had just experienced with the Church Board.

Reaching for the switch on his nightstand lamp, Paul rose from the bed. "If you really want to know about it, I'll tell you all the gory details. First let me take something for this headache." Susan waited anxiously while he fumbled through the medicine cabinet looking for aspirin. After a moment or so he found some and went down to the kitchen, where he downed two tablets. After what seemed like an eternity to Susan, he returned and climbed back into bed.

"For starters, Larry Lyons is not coming to church anymore," he blurted out as he pulled the sheet up over himself. He knew the news would hurt Susan as deeply as it did himself.

"You're kidding—not Larry! He was the chairman of the pulpit committee!"

"Larry blames himself for his role in calling me to the church. When the ministry was going well he took the credit for his wise decision, but now he's getting too much feedback on his big mistake. I guess he's too weak to handle the criticism, so he quit coming."

"I knew he hadn't been out for awhile, but he told us he was going on vacation."

"He was only on vacation for one week. The last three weeks he hasn't gone anywhere to church. In fact my secretary saw him cutting his lawn last Sunday morning when she passed his house on her way to worship."

"Larry Lyons," Susan mused sadly. They both lay quietly in bed for awhile as the impact of Paul's report sank in.

Then she caught herself and mustered a more cheery voice. "At least there's the Jenkins family, Paul. They've been out to worship with us four weeks in a row."

"Don't count on it," he snapped.

"Why's that?"

"I called Mrs. Jenkins today to talk about church membership with her. I wanted to be able to tell the board tonight that her family was interested in joining the church."

"What did she say? Don't they want to join?"

"I'm afraid not. She told me their 'policy' is to visit a church for a whole month before deciding whether to join or to keep looking...."

"...and they've decided to keep looking?"

"They were satisfied with everything about our church—except the preaching. 'Preaching isn't a real love of yours, is it, Pastor Andrews?' " Paul quoted Mrs. Jenkins, mocking her high, nasal voice.

"Some people are so ignorant!" Susan exclaimed. She pounded the bed with her fist.

"The news about Larry Lyons and the Jenkins family ignited a heated discussion about my preaching. Evidentally the Board has been hearing lots of complaints about it lately."

"You must admit your heart hasn't been in it for some time," she replied. Her voice was uncondemning.

"I know it hasn't," Paul admitted. "Then Tom Fedderhoffer brought up the idea of having Dr. Mackey preach a series in our pulpit."

"Tom has requested that before."

"Yes, but tonight he really pushed for it, and he had the Board in agreement with him before the meeting was over. They tabled action until Tom could find out if 'Mac's' schedule would permit a several-week commitment. He's such a popular speaker. You know how Tom and 'Mac' are real close," Paul sighed sarcastically. Susan could hear the deep hurt in his voice.

"Oh, Paul, what are we going to do? Do you think it's time for us to find another church?"

"I don't know. It seems like it. I know I have to do something, but suppose I have the same problem in a new church? What will we do then? Uproot our family every time people get tired of my preaching? Maybe I should quit the ministry altogether, and sell cars or life insurance. That's about the only thing an ex-preacher is good for!"

Paul groaned and gripped his head tightly as a sudden stab of pain caught him by surprise.

"I hate the idea of moving, Paul. I love our home. Our kids are so happy with the Christian school. This community is perfect for raising our family."

"I know. I feel the same way, but I don't know what to do about it."

Glancing at the clock, Paul noticed that it now read 1:35 A.M.

"I guess I better get some sleep. I have that 6:15 appointment with our Sunday school superintendent." He reached up and turned out the light on his nightstand.

A few minutes passed, then Susan broke the dark silence. "Honey, it will be okay."

The quiet confidence in her voice made Paul forget about himself for the first time all evening. He reached for her hand.

"You never cease to amaze me. Having a pastor for a husband is not the easiest calling in the world!"

"I must admit I sometimes wish you were a dentist or an ophthalmologist, but being a pastor's wife isn't so bad. Besides, what did you tell me Spurgeon said about preachers?"

"He said, 'If God calls you to preach the gospel, don't stoop along the way to become a king.' "

"That makes me a step above queen, so why should I be sorry my husband's a minister?"

"Well, my dear queen, those words were much more inspiring back in seminary. Tonight they sound rather hollow."

"They'll sound better again tomorrow, Paul."

"I don't know about that, but thanks for listening and being so kind. The last thing I needed tonight was more criticism."

"That's okay. Anytime you need pastoral counseling, just come to my office," she teased.

2

The Return of Dr. Vickerson

Paul was only three minutes late for his breakfast appointment. It was during breakfast that he noticed the day's date in his appointment book: June 4. While Glenn went on about the troubles in the Sunday school department, Paul's mind drifted back to the events that took place exactly ten years before. This was the tenth anniversary of his ordination. Ten years ago he began his work at Calvary Church. Ten years to the day the church officers laid hands on him and set him apart for the ministry. What a difference between then and now!

Glenn kept talking; Paul kept drifting. He watched Glenn's lips move and gave an occasional nod, but his thoughts were centered now on that special time ten years in the past.

Then Glenn made a remark that caught his attention.

"Pastor, some of our Sunday school teachers have been complaining that they're tired of teaching. I practically have to beg them to stay on for one more year. I don't know whether you can appreciate what it's like for these teachers to prepare a new lesson week after week."

"Oh, I think I can identify with that problem very well," Paul interjected.

"You can? Did you teach Sunday school once?"

"No, but there's the matter of the weekly sermon," Paul smiled.

He secretly thought, "Funny, if the teachers get stale we beg them to stay, but if the pastor's preaching gets old, they threaten to kick him out!"

"I never thought about the sermon that way," Glenn continued. "Anyway, Linda Swanson feels so burned out that she made me promise she'd be the first teacher I'd replace. But I don't know who to ask in her place.

"Pastor, there—is—a difference, you know."

"What do you mean?"

"Well, yours is a full-time salaried position. The people expect you to work hard and stay fresh. But these teachers are only volunteers. How can I expect that of them?"

"I know what you're saying, Glenn, and you're right about me. But I can't imagine our Sunday school teachers standing before the Lord someday and saying, 'But, God, I was—only—a volunteer! What did you expect of me?'"

"I see what you mean, Paul. I guess we're all to do our work 'heartily as unto the Lord.'"

Suddenly the superintendent glanced at his watch, grabbed the check, and quickly rose from the table. "I didn't realize how late it's getting. I'll take care of breakfast. Bye!"

As Paul waved goodbye to Glenn an idea flashed through his mind: "Why not drive over to the seminary? It's not that far away."

Paul didn't feel like hearing about another complaint, another person leaving the church, another problem. So he jumped into his old white Dodge and rumbled off toward the school. Coincidentally, it was in the opposite direction from the church office.

The drive was pleasant. The sun was shining and the temperature was 74 degrees. The sky was bright blue, with just enough cottony clouds to make for a perfect day. As he neared the school, Paul could hardly believe how much better he was feeling already. Even the headache from the night before had left him.

He pulled into the main parking area next to the administration building. The seminary grounds featured thick grass lawns trimmed everywhere with a variety of summer flowers adding their red, yellow, white, and violet colors. Mighty oak trees reached their limbs toward the heavens, while their leaves brought cool shade to the lawns beneath.

The campus was quiet: Summer school wouldn't begin for another week. Paul counted only three people making their ways between the various buildings.

The fact that so few were there did not dampen his joyous mood at all. To the contrary, it was a relief to think that no one would recognize him and start asking the usual questions, such as "How are things going with your ministry?"

The administrative building was occupied by some of the secretarial staff. He recognized a few familiar faces and waved but did not stop to talk.

He paused long enough to read the bulletin board notices. Blue cards indicating vacant churches were neatly arranged according to denominational affiliation. It was on this same board that Paul had first seen the notice for Calvary Church. A slight tinge of excitement surged through him as he searched the list of vacancies.

Suddenly he caught himself. "What am I thinking about? I don't really want to leave Calvary. I may be forced to move, but I don't want to."

After a drink of cold water from the fountain he had frequented during his seminary days, Paul left the building. He paused long enough for his eyes to readjust to the bright sunlight, then headed in the direction of the library. Again the grounds were empty of students and faculty.

As Paul entered the library he was confronted by a strange new gadget installed at the doorway. He cautiously stepped around it, and as he did, it emitted a quiet clicking noise.

"That's a security gate," an unfamiliar voice answered his puzzled look. "It sounds an alarm if anyone attempts to remove a library book without properly checking it out."

"What an odd need for a Christian school," Paul muttered to himself.

"What's that?" The new librarian asked. Her voice was uncharacteristic of the stereotypic library whisper.

"It just seems strange to need a security gate in a seminary library—especially a Christian seminary!" Paul said more loudly.

"You'd be surprised. We've even caught professors walking out with books hidden inside their briefcases," she said with an ominous official tone.

"Don't worry about me!" Paul laughed, raising his hands in mock surrender. "I have enough troubles without spending 10 to 20 in the slammer for library theft!"

As he started toward the ground floor stacks, she pounced from behind the desk and stopped him dead in his tracks.

"You'll have to identify yourself before I can admit you, sir."

He soon convinced her of his alumnus status and was issued a temporary pass.

"As a former student of this seminary you are welcome to make free and full use of the library anytime you wish," she explained with a professional air. "You may pick up your permanent library card as you leave today."

Armed with his new badge of authority, Paul was now permitted to browse through the old familiar stacks again. He chuckled to himself at the dramatic encounter with the young librarian.

He had no particular game plan in mind as he meandered back and forth among the ground floor shelves.

Beside the librarian and one assistant, Paul was beginning to think he was the only other person there. He ascended a flight of marble stairs to the second floor. Then, as he rounded the corner at the top of the steps, he spied his favorite lounge area adjacent to the stairwell.

Paul quickened his pace toward the room, his eye fixed on the pot of fresh coffee brewing inside. Because this was the only place in the library the students were allowed to eat and drink, he had made good use of it during his three years.

He was so preoccupied with the thought of a fresh cup of coffee that he failed to notice the wooden cane extending out from its resting place against the arm of a brown leather lounge chair. Paul stumbled over the cane, but he managed to catch himself from falling. The cane slammed onto the carpet with a dull thud.

As Paul looked back at the cane he realized that a familiar old friend was seated in the lounge chair.

"Dr. Vickerson!" he shouted as he straightened and turned to face the old man. "Dr. Vickerson, do you remember me? Paul Andrews? I had you for homiletics back about 12 or 13 years ago.

"I hope I didn't damage your cane," Paul apologized as he stooped to retrieve it.

The old man smiled broadly and rose slowly from his seat. His arthritic condition had worsened considerably over the last dozen years, turning simple movements into painful labors.

"Why, Paul, I do remember you. You were one of my favorite students. Of course I remember you." Dr. Vickerson extended a frail hand in order to grasp and shake Paul's hand. "I even remember the excellent sermon you preached in chapel. It was on the body of Christ and taken from 1 Corinthians 12."

"I'm surprised you even recognized me, yet alone remember my preaching," Paul laughed. "My hair is a little thinner, and my glasses and waistline are both a little thicker these days."

"Nonsense, you're still a youngster! If you want to see old, just look at me!"

Dr. Vickerson paused for a moment, then added, "I also remember another student in your class, a close friend of yours."

"You mean Barry Longstreet."

"Yes, that's it! Barry Longstreet. How's Barry doing these days?"

"I'm afraid he dropped out of the ministry about five years ago. The last I heard he was selling insurance."

"I'm sorry to hear that. Barry was so gifted. He had so much potential, but that often happens when a man thinks he can get by on his gifts alone," Dr. Vickerson observed.

"Dr. Vickerson, what are you doing here? I mean, I thought the year you taught me was your last year? Didn't you move to Phoenix because of your health?" Paul could hardly contain his joy at seeing his old teacher.

"You remember all that about me?" Dr. Vickerson answered in his characteristic humble fashion.

"The move to Arizona was a big mistake. The improvement to my back and joints was hardly noticeable, but what I did notice was the way that the dry, dusty air affected my lungs and bronchial passages. I nearly died out there trying to breath. After a few years Emily and I moved to Florida, but the humidity and heat were unbearable. When Emily died a few months ago I decided to come back here to live."

"I still remember your beautiful brick home over on Elmhurst Street. Where do you live now?" Paul asked.

"That was a beautiful house, wasn't it?" Dr. Vickerson's voice choked with sorrow. He paused to clear his throat. "I have a small apartment over in the senior citizens' high-rise on Sixth Street."

"That's still close to the school," Paul remarked. "How often do you come over here?"

"Quite frankly, not often. A colleague of mine has been after me to read his latest book on homiletics. I came here to look at the seminary's copy. I think he expected me to buy my own, but why does an old man like me need a new book on preaching? I thought I'd skim through it while I was here today."

"Maybe I need to buy that book," Paul tried to laugh as he said it.

"What do you mean? You're a good preacher, young man!"

"Thanks, Dr. Vickerson, but that isn't exactly what my congregation thinks. I've been getting lots of complaints lately. Last night Susan and I even talked about moving to another church. I hate the thought of it, but right now I think I might not have much choice in the matter." Paul glanced down at the floor and shuffled his feet self-consciously as he spoke.

"Paul, there is an alternative to moving."

"What's that? Selling insurance for Barry?" Paul laughed weakly.

"No! Of course not! It's staying right where you are and pumping some freshness and new life back into your preaching. If you move you might end up repeating the same pattern at another church. No, I think you ought to stay right where you are. Work on your preaching. Improve it. Revitalize it."

Somehow his words seemed encouraging, but Paul protested.

"Dr. Vickerson, I may have to move. My congregation may not be so patient with a ten-year veteran of the ministry. They probably think I should have figured this preaching out by now."

"Nonsense, son, you're still young! You have a lot to learn yet about the ministry. Too many young preachers leave the seminary fired with enthusiasm and vision, only to lose it all after a few short years. That freshman spirit might get you through your beginning years in the parish, but sooner or later you must learn how to catch a second wind. The ministry is not a hundred-yard dash; it's a marathon! Young Timothy hadn't been at work too long before the apostle had to encourage him to rekindle his gift! Right?"

"Dr. Vickerson, do you really think there's hope for my preaching? It's so stale, so old. My people have a right to complain. I think if I were a member of my church I'd want to leave too!"

"Of course there's hope for your preaching. You can rekindle that spark and bring new freshness and life to the pulpit. Believe me, Paul." Dr. Vickerson rested his hand on Paul's shoulder as he spoke. "Your people will see the difference too."

You must learn how to catch a second wind. The ministry is not a hundred-yard dash; it's a marathon!

His face radiated confidence as he spoke. It was the medicine Paul needed to build up his spirit again, and he was suddenly seized with a thought: Dr. Vickerson might be an answer to his prayers.

"Dr. Vickerson, are you busy these days? I'm sorry, I know you are a busy man. What I mean is, can you find the time to help me with my preaching, kind of like a tutorial?"

"Paul, I would love to help out. What if we get together early each week to discuss your sermon from the Sunday before?"

"That would be wonderful! I can't wait to get started."

"Great! Then let's begin next week. How about Monday morning at my apartment, 10:00 A.M.?"

"Monday morning 10 o'clock will be fine!"

Paul filled two cups for the professor and himself. As they sipped the fresh coffee the two talked a little longer. Then Paul made his way back down the stairs toward the front door and the professor returned to his colleague's book.

Passing through the library detector, Paul experienced a strange relief that the alarm didn't go off. Again, all he heard was the quiet ticking noise.

"Wait!" a loud cry stopped him as he opened the front door.

The librarian raced around the front desk and out to the door. "You forgot your new library card!" she exclaimed as she handed it to him.

"Oh, of course. Thank you very much!" Paul smiled as he studied his name on the laminated card.

"Be sure to put it to good use now," she added. "Too many of our alumni never take advantage of their library as they should."

"I will. I'll be sure to do that. In fact, I may see you next week," Paul laughed.

As he headed for home it seemed that somehow the skies were even brighter than before.

"Perhaps there is hope for a tired, burned-out preacher like me," he thought, recalling the assurances Dr. Vickerson gave him. Inside he began to wonder how long it would be before he could catch that second wind.

3

The Preacher's One Business

Monday morning came too soon. The week had gone by quickly since the meeting in the library. In the dimly lighted hallway outside the apartment Paul hesitated, then knocked. A voice from inside invited him in.

As he opened the door the odor of fresh paint greeted him. He stood momentarily in the entryway and surveyed the apartment before him. For the most part it was simple and uncluttered. Each room was painted with a fresh coat of white paint. As he stepped into the living room he noticed white cords located in several places along the base of the walls.

"Those are in case I fall and need to call for help." Dr. Vickerson seemed to be reading Paul's thoughts as he watched him survey the place. "They are a great comfort to those of us who live alone."

Until Paul heard him speak, he had not noticed Dr. Vickerson sitting at the table in the dinette area that opened up at the opposite end of the living room.

"Good morning, Dr. Vickerson. Sorry I'm late. I guess I underestimated the time it would take to get here."

This wasn't the only apology Paul had been rehearsing on the way over in his car.

Dr. Vickerson gestured for him to join him at the table. In the center of it a clear pitcher of ice tea was collecting moisture from the summer air. Beads of water trickled down the sides of the glass, forming tracks through the condensation. Next to the pitcher were two glasses of ice and some lemon slices.

"Make yourself at home and have some ice tea, Paul. I see you remembered to bring your materials with you."

Paul's face flushed. "Well, for what they're worth, but I didn't have much time to prepare yesterday's sermon. In fact, it was pretty bad."

"What kept you so busy last week?"

Paul had his excuse well-rehearsed: "Monday was our monthly board meeting. Tuesday I spent most of the day down here. That's when I met you in the library. Wednesday and Thursday were taken up with administrative matters, getting the bulletin ready for the secretary, and various phone interruptions. Friday morning, as I began to work on the sermon, I got an emergency call from the North Area Medical Center. One of our shut-ins had suffered a stroke."

"That hospital's a good distance from your place."

"Mrs. Simpson has been living across town with her daughter for several years now, but the family still expects me to visit her every few months. She was a charter member of our church and they remind me of that fact every time I see them. By the time I got back it was after lunch, so I visited a few members and called it a day. I spent Saturday with my family, since I hadn't seen them all week long."

"When did you work on your sermon?"

"I started on it around 9:00 o'clock Saturday night, after the children went to bed."

Dr. Vickerson flinched as Paul continued to explain.

"I worked till 12:30, then got up two hours earlier on Sunday to finish it up. You can see the results of my efforts on this sheet."

He pulled out a crinkled sheet of paper that had been stuffed in his Bible, and he handed it to the old professor. Dr. Vickerson unfolded the paper and began to study its contents. He squinted at the writing, tilting the paper at an angle, as if it might help him discern a few of the more illegible words.

Paul's embarrassment deepened. A phrase of Scripture he had memorized as a child in Sunday school suddenly flashed through his mind: "a workman that needeth not to be ashamed." Dr. Vickerson laid the outline down and reached for his ice tea. His thin hand trembled as he raised the glass to his lips. After a long drink he slowly set his glass down. He looked at Paul kindly and began to speak.

"Preaching, in order to be fresh and vital, takes hard work. The work can be quite agonizing at times. In fact, the longer you are in the ministry the more discipline and determination is needed to accomplish the work. That is an important principle to remember. I would write it down in your notes if I were you. *The longer you are in the ministry, the more disciplined effort it takes to preach with freshness and vitality.*"

By now Paul's face burned hot with shame, so he welcomed the opportunity to avoid eye contact. He opened the notebook that Dr. Vickerson had asked him to bring and buried his head in it as he began to write.

"Paul, can you remember what we talked about on the very first day in homiletics class? I asked all of you to underline the first few verses of Acts 6. It was dealing with the apostles setting up what some believe to have been the first board of deacons in the church."

"Yes, I remember underlining those verses in my old Bible, but two years ago I had to buy a new one."

"Well, open your Bible to Acts 6 and underline those verses again."

Paul underlined Acts 6:2,4 in his New American Standard Bible:

> It is not desirable for us to neglect the word
> of God in order to serve tables. . . . But we will
> devote ourselves to prayer, and to the ministry
> of the word.

"This ministry is always at odds with the Prince of Darkness," Dr. Vickerson continued. "He will do anything to subvert your work. He will have you running here and there doing a thousand good little works in order to keep you from doing those two important works: prayer and the ministry of the Word. All your efforts should run toward those two aspects of ministry. Nothing you do should detract from it. This is your calling, your 'job description,' if you like.

"I realize that I'm a professor and you are a preacher. Professors are thought to be the idealists and preachers the realists, but the week you just described to me had little to do with your real calling to prayer and the ministry of the Word."

Paul was growing defensive. He could already think of a dozen excuses for those thousand little works that kept him from his high calling, but for the moment he kept silent as the professor continued.

"Henry Ward Beecher once delivered an address at the Yale Lecture Series which he entitled 'Preaching: the Preacher's Whole Business.' Listen to what he says about our human limitations."

Dr. Vickerson opened his black leather notebook. Turning to one of its yellowed pages, he read the words he had neatly entered by hand years before:

There is not one of you who was built large enough to do anything more than [preach]. . . . A man who is going to be a successful preacher should make his whole life run toward the pulpit. . . . When a man stands in the pulpit, and all the streams run away from the pulpit down to those other things, the pulpit will be very shallow and very dry; but when a man opens these streams in the neighboring hills as so many springs, and all the streams run down into the pulpit, he will have abundant supplies. . . . Then he is not carrying out three or four businesses at the same time. He is carrying on *one business*; and he collects from a hundred the materials and forces by which he does it.

Dr. Vickerson paused and looked into Paul's face, then spoke with great emphasis: "One business: the business of preaching. That is all any man is big enough to do if he is to do it well."

The Prince of Darkness will have you running here and there doing a thousand good little works in order to keep you from doing those two important works: prayer and the ministry of the Word.

Paul began his protest: "But that's unrealistic! My church expects me to drive across town to make hospital calls, to visit in their homes, to lead the board meetings, to carry out the administrative details, to serve in community affairs, to—"

"Wait—wait one minute!" Dr. Vickerson interrupted. "That, my friend, is what's unrealistic. No man is big enough to do all those things and to do them well. Beecher wasn't saying to do nothing but preach. He was saying that everything else you do must have preaching as its target. In his own metaphor those other things must be streams flowing down to the pulpit rather than flowing away from the pulpit."

Dr. Vickerson took a sheet of paper from Paul's note book and sketched the two different ways to view preaching. One was a reservoir with all the streams flowing out and away from it, and the other was a reservoir with all the streams converging upon it.

"Do you see the difference between the two?" He asked. "The one drains everything *away from* your task of preaching. It runs you dry. The other channels everything *toward* your preaching, constantly filling the reservoir with resources and energies to carry out the work. There is an enormous difference."

"It sounds like you're asking me to rearrange my whole life—my whole schedule—if I'm to find that freshness and vitality I've lost through the years. Is that how I'll find the time to 'fill up the reservoir,' to use your analogy?"

"Yes, and I *am* probably asking you to rearrange your whole schedule. For ten years now the streams of your ministry have been flowing away from the pulpit, not toward it. You are drained by your work."

Dr. Vickerson noticed a hurt look in Paul's eyes, but he quickly went ahead. "Anyone would be drained by it, Paul. The Lord knows there are thousands of preachers out there who are exhausted and disheartened. Most of them hit the ministry running full-steam-ahead the first year out of seminary, but within a few years they're run-down and out of steam. To use Beecher's analogy, their reservoirs have run dry. Many of them drop out of the ministry. You know that better than I, if you've kept in touch with your classmates."

"Like Barry Longstreet. Looking back on it, I see your point. When Barry graduated from seminary, he was full of enthusiasm about the ministry. I guess he just ran dry after four or five years."

"A perfect example. Barry was probably the best young preacher I ever had in my homiletics classes. He was full of potential. But you don't survive in the ministry on potential.

"Preaching is one of the most difficult jobs I know. It demands everything of the preacher. It takes hard, agonizing work—not physical work, but mental and spiritual anguish that comes from the struggle against satanic powers and principalities. Biblical preaching is a declaration of war on the kingdom of darkness. Satan does not sit idly by. When he finds someone who is diligently faithful to the ministry of prayer and the Word, he goes on the attack."

"Dr. Vickerson, what should I do? How do I get started? For one thing, I have ten years of habits and schedules that my people are accustomed to. They expect me to keep doing the things I've always done. It seems like the only answer is to leave the church and start all over again somewhere else." His voice reflected frustration and despair.

"No, you don't need to find a new church; just find a new way of doing ministry *right where you are*. But first you must rededicate yourself to a wholehearted commitment to preaching. It must become your one great priority. You must determine to be fresh and alive in the pulpit. You must determine to deliver well-prepared messages."

"I want to, but it still seems so unrealistic."

"Think of prayer and the ministry of the Word as two great filters through which all your other tasks must pass. Instead of making decisions about what jobs will please your members, filter those decisions on the basis of what you must do to please *God*. Everything must pass through the filter of prayer and the ministry of the Word. Everything."

Dr. Vickerson waited momentarily while his words sank in. Paul sat silently across the table, imagining all the changes and challenges such a commitment would take.

"Are you willing to commit yourself to it, Paul? I know you're concerned about how your people will react if you cut back in some other areas of your ministry to do this, but I'm more concerned about your Lord. When you stand before Him to account for your work... for work like this (he reached for Paul's sermon outline and held it up), what excuse will you give your Master for it?"

Dr. Vickerson's words stung, even worse than Mrs. Jenkins' telephone conversation the week before. But they were necessary. The medicine tasted bitter, but the loving-kindness of the old man made it easier for Paul to swallow.

"Preaching is not only your *high* calling, Paul, but it is your *whole* calling. Preaching is the preacher's whole business. Are you willing to commit yourself to that?"

Dr. Vickerson's insistence on commitment reminded Paul of a Billy Graham invitation. He felt like the choir was somewhere in the fourth verse of "Just As I Am." If he didn't go forward soon, the song would be over. Paul thought to himself, "Not just the music, but maybe the ministry will be finished."

After a long pause he broke the silence and asked, "How do I get started, Dr. Vickerson?"

"I have an idea. Let's go to lunch. I'll buy! Does your schedule allow you to have lunch with me?"

Dr. Vickerson's abrupt change in the conversation came as a relief to Paul. He felt like a patient who had just awakened from the anesthetic to learn that surgery had already been completed.

"How can I turn down an offer like that!" he brightened. "But first I'll have to cancel an appointment for this afternoon. The chairperson of the Women's Association is coming in to discuss plans to remodel the lounge. She wants to know what I think of the drapes she picked out."

"See, you're already straightening out your priorities—dinner with the Doctor instead of deliberating over the draperies!"

They both laughed as Paul got up to make his phone call.

"Young man, do you realize that within the next few months you are going to become a different preacher . . . that things are going to really change in your life? You and your people are going to recognize some important changes!"

Paul looked at the professor. He saw the twinkle and excitement in Dr. Vickerson's eyes, shining out from behind his wire-rimmed bifocals. His remarks both puzzled and excited Paul. He stood watching the professor, anticipating that he might say more to elaborate on what those changes might be.

"Hurry up and make that phone call!" Dr. Vickerson continued as he gestured toward the telephone. "I'm getting hungry!"

4

The Importance of Starting Early

Dr. Vickerson's choice of restaurant surprised Paul—he didn't expect Italian. After placing his order from a large laminated menu, Paul looked over the place. It hadn't changed much since seminary days. There were the same old red-and-white checkered tablecloths, the same green lampshades suspended over each booth and table, and even the same red paint on the ceiling overhead.

"I hope you don't mind eating here." The Doctor interrupted Paul's perusal of the place.

"Not at all! This was our favorite restaurant back when I was in school. I must admit, though, I never pictured you eating pizza in an Italian restaurant."

Dr. Vickerson laughed as he replied. "Don't tell anyone, Paul, but after we're done eating I'm going to take home part of the pizza and keep it for breakfast. Cold pizza for breakfast is much tastier than bacon and eggs."

"Isn't it amazing," Paul observed, "how the food in a little place like this is often so much better than the food in an expensive restaurant where you pay for all that atmosphere."

"Same with preachers." Dr. Vickerson seized the opportunity to get back to the business at hand. "Some have all the right 'atmosphere' surrounding their messages, but when you examine the content of the spiritual food they offer, it's terrible."

"Back in seminary Barry Longstreet used to tell us about a preacher in one of the prestigious churches downtown. Barry would say, 'He says nothing, very well.'"

"That's often the case, but be careful not to ignore their methods. These people often master techniques, even though they never do say anything of eternal substance and value. Study their methods, Paul. Learn from the liberal preachers in the areas in which they excel. Often those who hold a high view of God's Word mistakenly think they don't need to do the diligent work of sermon preparation. They just throw out the message to the people in whatever form it first comes to them."

"For example," Dr. Vickerson continued. "how would you react if the waitress brought your meal today uncooked and unassembled? First course: raw pizza dough. Next, tomatoes for the sauce, raw onions, green pepper, oregano leaves, etc. To top it off, some of your favorite uncooked sausage! How would you react?"

"I wouldn't eat it, that's for sure!"

"Exactly! Is it any wonder that your people often refuse to eat the spiritual food you serve? If a message is unprepared it is indigestible."

"I once heard another homiletics professor make the same point by using raw steak as the illustration." Paul observed. "He told an audience of preachers, 'Your wife can go to the butcher and buy the juiciest, most tender cut of steak in town, but if she just throws it on your plate raw and bloody, you aren't going to eat it! It has to be prepared in the best way possible in order to draw out the juicy taste of the beef."

"Of course! Only a cannibal would eat it that way! Here's your first secret of freshness, Paul: When exegesis and commentary study are finished, you must still do the even harder imaginative work of preparing the sermon from those raw ingredients."

> *Often those who hold a high view of God's Word mistakenly think they don't need to do the diligent work of preparation. They just throw out the message to the people in whatever form it first comes to them.*

Paul made a brief note in his writing tablet just as their steaming hot food arrived. Dr. Vickerson had ordered a medium pizza cut in six slices—three for now, three for breakfast. Paul had ordered a half-and-half plate with portions of lasagna and cheese ravioli.

For awhile the conversation stopped as the two eagerly dug into their food. The only remark came from Dr. Vickerson, who noted how good it felt not to eat alone.

After their initial craving was satisfied, the lessons resumed. Dr. Vickerson took his napkin, unfolded it, and began sketching a chart on it with his pen. Between bites of pizza he explained his drawing to Paul.

"Too many preachers get caught in the vicious circle of last-minute sermon preparation. The habit not only wastes their talents, but it harms the people of God. On top of that, it takes its toll on the physical and emotional makeup of the pastor."

He turned his napkin around for Paul to study it. Paul stopped eating and began copying the diagram in his notebook, making some explanatory notes underneath it.*

"The horizontal bar represents the days of the week starting Sunday evening and leading up to the following week's sermon. Notice the huge drop in tension after you finish preaching. You feel relieved and relaxed again. If the sermon was bad you might feel depressed, but the tension is gone."

Paul nodded as he continued copying.

"As the week progresses there is a natural buildup of tension until the Sunday deadline arrives. Usually we aren't aware of that tension growing inside until later in the week, but it actually starts again right after the initial letdown. Friday and Saturday it can skyrocket, especially in the person who begins to prepare at the last minute."

"I'm the perfect example of what you're describing. In fact, if I'm not well-prepared by Saturday night I often sleep very restlessly; sometimes I even have bizarre dreams."

"Naturally. Your body is tired but your mind is fighting it to stay awake in order to get that unfinished business done. Tell me about your dreams Paul."

"Almost always it involves my being unable to get dressed in time to get to the church. Sometimes I make it and sometimes I never get there. If I do succeed in getting there in time to preach I'll look down at myself as I stand in the pulpit, and realize I'm only partly dressed. Sometimes I'm wearing my shirt and tie but no pants!"

"I don't claim to be a Joseph, but it seems pretty obvious that your dreams are no mere coincidence. Being only partially dressed is related to your fear of standing in the pulpit only partially prepared."

"My wife says the same thing, and I have to agree. It only happens when I go to bed on Saturday night without a complete message in my mind."

*See chart on following page.

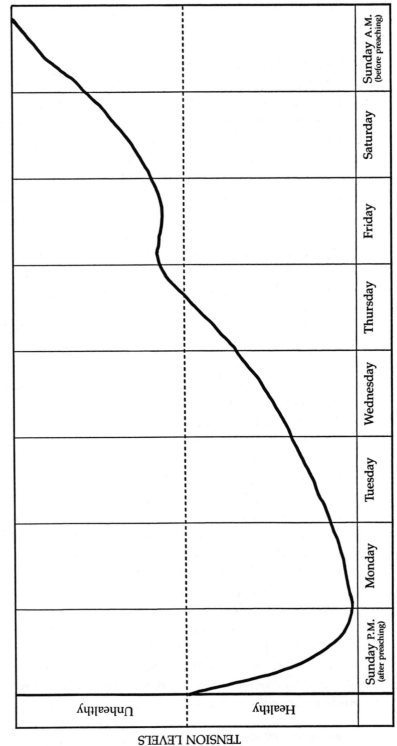

LATE STARTER'S TENSION CHART

"That's the very point I'm making by this little chart. Your mind is always at work, even when you're not consciously using it. Tension is a valuable energy. Like any other kind of energy, it can be harnessed for good or else it can gallop around unharnessed. Unharnessed, it will be destructive in all sorts of ways. That's why a late start harms both people and pastor. Some preachers end up in the hospital with ulcers, others with chest pains. Make no mistake—this vicious circle is *vicious*. Think of what it does to the preacher's family, too. How much attention and demonstration of loving concern is lost by pastoral preoccupations!"

"I know exactly what you mean, Dr. Vickerson. I'm the living example of everything you said."

"That's why you must break the circle. Attack early. Start on Monday or Tuesday—never later. That way you harness the natural tension inside you so that its energy is used productively. By starting early you also keep it under control so it doesn't jump off the charts at the end of each week, wreaking havoc in your body. Starting early is vitally important."

"Just how does an early start help to harness tension?" Paul asked.

"Think about your Saturday night dreams. All that energy is being directed toward the Sunday sermon. But because the sermon is ill-prepared, much of the energy is spent on worry rather than on the message itself."

"Look down at this second diagram." Dr. Vickerson pointed again to his napkin drawings.* "What happens if you do your exegesis on Monday instead of Saturday night or even Friday morning?"

"I guess your mind would then have something to work with all week long," Paul responded.

"Exactly! Instead of pouring your energies into a vacuum you pour them into the organization of a wealth of

*See chart on following page.

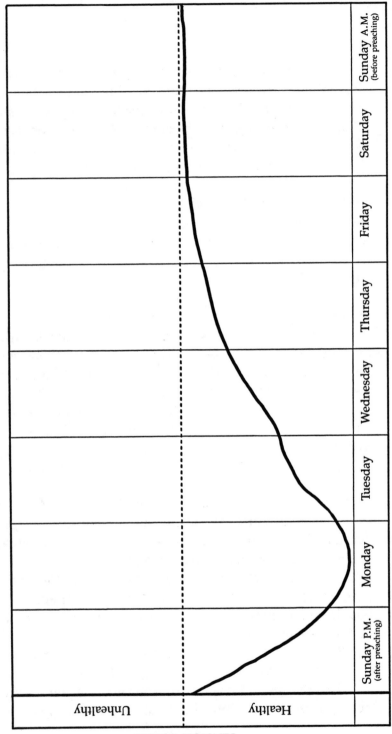

materials. Not only that, but the tension is a healthy, more relaxed tension. It's a good tension that says to your stomach and your insides, 'Don't worry, we have this under control. We have something to work with and we're working with it now!'"

Lights were going on in Paul. It was such a simple explanation. Why hadn't he seen it more clearly all along?

"So, Dr. Vickerson," Paul added, "as the week progresses the mind has something to mull over. I'm harnessing my natural energies to do the work they were begging me to do all along."

"Actually it's more than your natural energies that are doing the prompting, Paul. The Lord has anointed you by His Spirit to preach the Word. The Spirit prompts you to get to work early and do it well. Your own spirit is urged along by the Holy Spirit.

"One other thing, before I forget it: Early *exegesis* helps to prevent late *eisegesis*. You should write that down right across the top of that chart."

Paul said it aloud slowly as he wrote, "Early . . . exegesis . . . helps . . . prevent . . . late . . . eisegesis."

"Your sermon last week is a perfect example of what I mean by that." Dr. Vickerson waited long enough for Paul to finish writing to make that remark. He knew Paul would forget the sentence if he didn't.

Paul's face blushed an instant red. "What do you mean, sir?"

"You preached on gluttony, and you took it from Philippians 3:19 where it speaks of those 'whose god is their appetite.' Right?"

"Yes, I think the Bible is clear about gluttony being a sin." Paul was slightly flustered.

"I agree. I feel a little guilty right now in this Italian restaurant." Dr. Vickerson laughed to keep the rebuke mild. "But you need to do your homework on Philippians 3. The apostle was not talking about gluttony. He was talking about Judaizers who opposed the gospel and insisted on observing Old Testament dietary laws and circumcision in order to be saved. He goes on to say 'whose glory is in their shame.' I don't think that refers to gross immorality, as your sermon notes suggest. It refers to their taking pride in their circumcision."

There was a pause in the conversation as Dr. Vickerson smiled kindly at Paul. He continued, "You look puzzled. Trust me, Paul. I preached the same message myself once. Only I had the embarrassment of an angry confrontation with a very, shall we say, robust woman after church. She knew her Bible. She corrected me in front of the whole congregation. 'That doesn't refer to fat people! That refers to the Judaizers!' she snorted. Then she stomped out the door!"

"Did she ever come back?"

"As a matter of fact she did, but she was never too fond of me after that!" Dr. Vickerson laughed.

The two laughed together, then Paul returned to the theme of starting early: "Monday is usually my day off. Are you saying that I should change my day off?"

"Everyone is different. You'll have to decide that, but you might want to change it. Back when I was in the pastorate—"

"When were you in the pastorate, Dr. Vickerson?" Paul interrupted.

"My first eight years out of seminary I served in a small country parish. I wanted to taste firsthand what it meant to preach week after week before I took on the task of teaching in the seminary. Even when I was teaching I often served as an interim pastor in order to keep my hand in the fire!"

"That's really nice to know," Paul responded. "That must be why your understanding of the pastorate is so much better than some of the other professors I had back in school."

"I can't speak for my colleagues, but let me complete my thought. I had trouble taking Monday off because it tended to be a letdown day. I grumbled around the house every Monday until one day Emily said, 'Vic, why don't you go to work? If you can't enjoy your day off, don't take it!' "

"So you stopped taking days off?"

"No, I realized that if I got my sermon work done early in the week, I could enjoy the weekends much better. So I switched to Fridays, then went back to put the finishing touches on my sermons on Saturday. You should experiment with the week and see what suits you best."

"I usually don't feel like studying anything on Mondays, though. I can't imagine studying every Monday."

"You're studying now with me on Mondays! Besides, you're forgetting a key factor. The reason you don't feel like studying on Monday has a lot to do with all the cramming you did late Saturday night and Sunday morning. You're exhausted by Monday. But you'll break that vicious circle by starting early. You'll enter Sundays much more refreshed by having accomplished an early start on your work. Even that freshness will show up in your sermons. Your people will notice the difference.

"Attack early and attack daily!" Dr. Vickerson repeated. "You need to invest each day into your primary calling as a preacher of the gospel. Preaching is your business. Not only that, but you will find yourself settling into an attack-rest-attack-rest pattern. Each day will add more input and energy to your message. All week long you'll be filling up your reservoir, not draining it."

"There is one problem I see with your advice, though," Paul replied.

"What's that?"

"Well, I've often wasted the first half of my week trying to decide what I would be preaching on Sunday. Sometimes I study a passage for several hours, then lay it aside and search for another text to use."

"We homiletics professors all have fears that there are critters like you running around out there! Paul, don't you plan your preaching in advance?"

"Sometimes, if I'm preaching through a book, I have an idea what's coming up," Paul blushed. "But lots of times I don't start thinking about what I'll preach until after the Sunday before."

Attack early and attack daily! Each day will add more input and energy to your message. All week long you'll be filling up your reservoir, not draining it.

"I don't know how to say this, Paul, but let me explain to you how I planned and prepared my sermons. I don't want to hit you with too much too soon, but maybe you can file this away for future reference. Somewhere down the road you'll want to do this.

"After I switched days off from Monday to Friday," he continued as he began sketching on the blank page, "I decided to make all day Monday a day of reflection and sermon preparation—a day to reflect back on Sunday's sermon and service and a day to recharge my spiritual batteries. I set aside significant time for study and prayer.

"I played around with a reasonable schedule for sermon preparation. I finally settled into one in which I began to study three weeks in advance of each message I preached."

"Three weeks in advance!" Paul choked on a mouthful of Pepsi. "You call that 'reasonable'?"

"I told you I didn't want to hit you with too much too soon," Dr. Vickerson laughed. "But bear with me, son. I'm no prophet, but I predict that someday you'll be so committed to the priority of preaching that you'll be doing something similar to this yourself."

"Three weeks in advance," Paul repeated incredulously. "I'll believe that when I see it!"

"The first Monday I exegeted the passage. That's all I did that week with that particular passage. Then the second Monday I began to study various commentaries, parallel passages, and related materials. By the end of the second week I had outlined a preliminary sermon outline. The third week I fleshed out the outline with sermon illustrations and strong introductions and conclusions. I also used driving time in my car as practice time in which I preached portions of the message aloud to see how they sounded. On Saturday I usually stood at the pulpit and practiced through the message from start to finish."

"Yes, but Dr. Vickerson, I have to preach every week! I don't have the luxury of taking three weeks to prepare each sermon! Who preached for you the two weeks between your sermons?"

"I know you're teasing me, Paul," the old man smiled. "I actually worked on four sermons each week. The first Monday of the month I begin by reviewing the sermon I preached the day before. Even with all the advanced preparation, I tried to stay open to the Holy Spirit's leading. Often the sermon outline I prepared was not the exact message I preached. Insights would hit me even as I was preaching!

"I didn't want to forget what the Spirit had led me to say. So Monday morning I made additional notes to that effect on my sermon outline. Then I filed it away carefully for future reference. Don't throw away all that valuable work, Paul. You might be able to put it to good use—even 'repreach' old sermons on occasion."

"Repreach old sermons? Won't the people know?"

"Probably not, unless you use the same illustrations. Sometimes if you repeat an illustration in another sermon you get accused of preaching an old one. But preach an old sermon and change the illustrations, and no one will even notice!

"By the way, that is a great resource, especially on important occasions. Perhaps an event hits suddenly the day before you are to preach. You might be able to find an appropriate message and adapt it to the occasion. But we'll talk more about that at some later time."

Paul nodded in agreement at the comment to postpone. His mind was starting to swim a little with all that Dr. Vickerson had been sharing.

"So first I reviewed Sunday's message and then filed it away. Second, I did the exegesis on the message I would be preaching in three weeks.

"That's all I would do with that passage that week. The third thing I did was to begin the commentary study and various parallel passage studies for the sermon I would be preaching in two Sundays.

"I would do as much of that as I could that morning, then break away from my studies about 45 minutes to an hour before lunch. That time I reserved for prayer before the Lord."

"How did you handle interruptions?" Paul asked.

"Easy. I hid out at the seminary library, where I could control the interruptions. My wife knew how to reach me for emergencies, since I didn't have the luxury of a secretary to help out."

"And the people didn't mind your being away all day?"

"At first some complained, but I was able to lead them into an appreciation for why I did what I did. I told them they had their day of spiritual nourishment on Sundays, and I needed mine on Mondays. Not a day off, but a day of worship and study in God's Word.

"All week long I would work on that sermon, until I had shaped an appropriate outline for it. Then after lunch I began my work on the coming Sunday's message. I took the outline from my work the week before and began to search for ways to tighten it up and flesh it out."

"What do you mean by that?"

"Well, by tighten I mean to make the outline crisp, clear, smooth, and easy to follow. To flesh out I mean to find fitting illustrations and powerful words and phrases to communicate well the intent of the message. I found that in the afternoon I could work for a couple hours on it, then I would use the rest of the time to browse through some inspirational magazines, or take a walk around the campus to meditate and pray. I even made good use of the campus Ping-Pong table around midafternoon as a break from the mental work. That is, if I could find any takers."

"But when did you pick out the passages you'd actually preach on, Dr. Vickerson? Like I said before, I often spend hours just trying to decide what to preach."

"There's a simple solution to that problem, son. Not only will it reduce your tension level even further, but it will also aid you greatly in your gathering of illustrations and your overall sermon preparation.

"In fact it only takes two words to describe your solution: *Plan ahead.* In other words, *start even earlier!*"

"How in the world am I going to plan any further ahead?" asked the flustered student. "First it's start on Monday, then start three weeks in advance. Now what? Start a year ahead?"

"Exactly! How did you ever guess?"

"Just lucky," Paul groaned.

"Come on, it's not really that difficult a problem. What are the slowest times of your work year?"

"For me? I guess it's the summer months. A lot of the regular weekly events follow the school year. The summer schedule winds down a little— except for Bible School."

"So you take two or three weeks of time in July and tell your secretary and your Church Board that you're only available for emergencies. You hide out in some obscure place—like your old seminary library—and plan a whole year of sermons. Leave an emergency number for your wife and the secretary and bury yourself in your work."

"That sounds like another item I'll need to convince the Board is part of my calling."

"A vital part of your calling! First, take a little inventory on what you've preached over the last ten years at Calvary.

Look for areas you may have neglected. Then examine what you think are the needs of the church right now. Put the two together and search out the Scriptures for the sermons and sermon series you need to preach in the coming year.

"You won't have time to do all the exegesis for the whole year, but find one trustworthy commentary on the book of the Bible you plan to preach through in the coming year. Immerse yourself in the Bible and in that one commentary. As you study it, look for the natural divisions between sections of verses. Map them out with a calendar for the coming year in front of you. Try to think of an appropriate sermon title, or at least note the subject of the sermon. That will serve as a reminder to you during the coming year."

"What if I want to preach on a topical subject more than a verse-by-verse study?"

"Then you will have harder work to do. You'll need to make good use of a concordance and study out the various facets of Scripture on a certain topic. Try to see a pattern of sermons emerging from your listing of passages. Then seek out some trustworthy sources to study those passages you plan to use.

"Paul, if you want to go all-out on this, I suggest that you make a sheet with each week of the year on it. Remember to circle Sundays of special emphasis throughout the year so you aren't caught by surprise by them. Then make several columns: 'Date,' 'Scripture,' 'Topic,' 'Key Ideas', 'Suggested Hymns.' Keep the list in a prominent place throughout the year to remind yourself of where your preaching is headed. It will also keep you on the lookout for appropriate sermon illustrations. But we'll talk about illustrations more at some future time."

The time had come to pay the bill, and as they rose from the table Paul suddenly remembered Dr. Vickerson's remarks to him as he had called home to cancel his afternoon apointment. "Dr. Vickerson, you mentioned earlier that you were going to tell me how to break the news to my congregation about the changes that would be taking place. What did you mean by all that? Should I go back this week and announce to the congregation my new commitment to preaching?"

"Well, you better begin with your Board. But even before you do that you have some homework to do. We can talk about that on the way out to the car. First let me pay for our lunch."

Paul pulled out his wallet, but Dr. Vickerson insisted that it was his treat. Finally he agreed to let Paul leave the tip.

5

Redeeming the Time

Human beings have natural limitations. Arthritis manages to shrink those boundaries even more. As the two men slowly made their way back to the car, Dr. Vickerson paused every few steps to rest on his cane and regather strength and determination to go on.

He also used the resting moments to discuss the matter that intrigued Paul so much—talking to the Board about change.

"Paul, your Board has made it easier for you to discuss with them needed changes in your work."

"How's that?" Nothing about it sounded very easy to Paul.

Dr. Vickerson gave an impish look and began to explain his strategy. "They have made an issue of your preaching," he said. "Now you can go back to them with an attitude of

'I'm glad you brought up the subject. I have a few concerns myself that I would like us to address.' "

"What exactly are those concerns?" Paul asked.

He had to wait for a reply, as Dr. Vickerson had begun again to take a few more painful steps toward the parking lot. Paul had offered to pick him up at the door, but the professor declined. He forced himself to walk whenever possible in order to keep operable whatever movement his joints had left in them.

Pausing again, he began answering Paul's question while resting on his old wooden cane.

"First, you'll have to do some homework before you know exactly what your concerns are. It will be necessary for you to spend the next two weeks keeping close track of your schedule. Take a sheet of paper for each day and divide it into four columns. In the first column write 'Time'; in the second write 'Activity'; in the third 'I Should Do'; and in the last column 'Others Should Do'. Be sure to write down *every* activity throughout the day or you will miss some important clues. Every few hours stop to update your log. Don't wait till the end of the day or the next morning."

"I'm beginning to see your strategy. You want me to gather data so I can demonstrate to the Board those areas where I need to find other people to do the work. That way I can be free to carry out my real calling—prayer and the ministry of the Word."

"That's the plan. After all, what use will it be to learn the principles of fresh preaching if you never have time to use them? Knowing what to do but not having time to do it will only add to your discouragement. You must break that vicious circle. Right now you're spending too much time doing many good things and not enough time doing the one *best* thing that you've been called to do! Remember, the first step to fresh preaching is making the commitment to do whatever it takes to get there."

As they walked on to the car, Paul couldn't help notice the determination and commitment it took for Dr. Vickerson to get there. He also noticed the grimace on the old man's face as he carefully positioned himself beside the car door, then fell slowly backward into the seat. After angling his cane down the middle of the front seat, he pulled his right leg into the car, than leaned over to his left to avoid the car door as Paul closed it.

The summer sun trapped inside the car had heated it like an oven. Paul quickly started the engine and turned on the air conditioner, thankful that he had finally found the time to have it charged on Saturday. "Time," he thought to himself, "always trying to find the time..."

"I see a problem with your plan, Dr. Vickerson. I often have different commitments at different times of the year. The summer is a little slower for me. That's one reason I could find time to meet with you. But in other seasons my schedule might be totally unlike the one I keep these next two weeks."

"Ideally you should do this study at a more 'normal' time during your calendar year. But you can still gain important insight even now. One thing you can do to supplement your study is to make a 'through-the-year list' of your various activities and commitments. Think of the special emphasis that each season brings."

"Then I can do the same thing with that list in terms of things I should do and things that other people can and should be doing."

"Right. If I were you I would look back through your calendars from the last two years to compile that list. Don't trust your memory too much. Do you still have those calendars around, Paul?"

"Yes, I file them each year with my IRS papers. It'll be no problem to dig them out of the files."

Paul pulled out of the parking lot and began the five minute drive back to the professor's apartment.

"There are a few things you need to remember about the problem of people getting tired of a person's preaching," Dr. Vickerson said, taking these few moments to bring their first session to a conclusion.

"When you began your work ten years ago you were fresh out of seminary—fresh from three years of intensive study in theology, church history, Scripture, and the biblical languages. Your spiritual reservoir was full of the Word of God, full of ideas for sermons, full of special messages and exciting illustrations you could hardly wait to use."

"Not only that," the professor continued, "but you were full of inexperience! That lack of confidence and experience drove you to work all the harder on the weekly sermon. Most of us started out in the ministry with the fear that we'd run out of things to say after the first seven minutes of a 25-minute message. You probably studied and prepared harder and longer for the sermon during those early years than you ever have since."

"You're right about that. I spent about 45 hours on one sermon the first month in my church. Not long ago I spent a whole 45 minutes preparing!"

"It should almost be just the opposite. The longer you are in the same place the more deliberately you must work to preach with freshness. You have to dig deeper in order to say more and say it differently. Don't try to rely on the inspiration of the moment. That is gambling on the Spirit of God to pick up the slack in your preparation. There is a big difference between preaching in faith that relies on the Spirit and preaching that gambles on the Spirit.

"The other thing that happens to the young preacher as time goes by, Paul, is that a certain smoothness comes with the experience of the years. That smoothness has a more professional sound to it, but it may also bring with it a certain dullness. There's nothing that keeps you more alert than listening to unpolished young preachers. You never know what will come out of their mouths next! That's one of the reasons I found homiletics so enjoyable. It's much more fun than listening to all those smooth talking professionals."

Dr. Vickerson's accent on the word "professionals" showed his disdain for the term so popular in certain ministry circles. When they reached the apartment Paul parked the car and opened the back door to retrieve Dr. Vickerson's pizza box from the back seat. He helped his professor out of the car and accompanied him into the elevator inside the main entrance lobby.

As time goes by a certain smoothness comes with the experience of the years. That smoothness has a more professional sound to it, but it may also bring with it a certain dullness.

As the elevator ascended to the fourth floor, Dr. Vickerson continued: "A few years out of seminary and that reservoir runs dry, usually about the same time the enthusiasm for the ministry starts to wane. It's a deadly combination, leaving the preacher with little left to say and even less desire to say it. So he starts to struggle with whether it's time to leave."

The elevator door opened and the two stepped out into the hallway. The apartment was the first one beyond the elevator. As Dr. Vickerson reached for his keys he concluded.

"Then guess what happens, Paul."

"The minister accepts a call to another congregation."

"Right. And when he gets to the new church he's enthusiastic and they're enthusiastic. His preaching is fresh and new to them, not like the preacher's that just left. But what they don't know is that the new minister is not saying anything new and fresh at all; he's merely repeating himself from his prior ministry. He's being very repetitious, but they haven't been around him long enough to hear the repetition yet!"

"So for awhile the ministry is new and fun again, then the same pattern repeats itself," Paul mused. "That's the very reason I've hesitated in moving for so long. I keep thinking that the problem will pack itself up and move with me."

"It will, Paul, it will. That's why you must break the vicious circle here and now, right where you are—not just for your sake, but for the people too, and especially for the glory of God! For too long the church has been plagued with ministers who repeat their three-year ministries six times in six different churches. Instead of 18 years of experience in the ministry, they really only have three years repeated six times. It's a terrible problem that has greatly harmed the cause of Christ in the world. It has to be stopped, Paul. In your life it has to be stopped."

When they entered the apartment, Paul set the pizza on the lower shelf of the refrigerator. There was plenty of room for it in the half-empty refrigerator. Paul remembered how packed with food it used to be back when Mrs. Vickerson was entertaining the students. The standard saying was "Look out below!" whenever someone opened the refrigerator, since something was always sure to spill out and hit the linoleum floor with a hard thud. Mrs. Vickerson had even broken her big toe once with a pound of frozen ground beef!

Dr. Vickerson turned to Paul and said, "Remember to keep an accurate chart these next two weeks. You need to gather your data for the Church Board. Also, don't forget your promise to me—and to the Lord—to determine to preach differently, to get out of the rut, to say things with newness, freshness, and new vitality!"

Paul could hardly believe their time together had ended. He was so eager to learn that he didn't want to leave. "Dr. Vickerson, it's only 1:30. Since I canceled that appointment this afternoon, I don't need to be home until 5:30 for dinner. I could stay awhile longer, if you don't mind."

"Sorry, Paul, but you don't have time to stay longer. You have too much to do!"

"What do you mean?" asked Paul, taken back by his response.

"Paul, you've already forgotten one of our first lessons: Start early! Remember, early exegesis helps you to avoid late eisegesis. Don't forget that little diagram I drew for you in the restaurant. Start today to harness the tension that's already building within you. Make it work *for* you instead of *against* you. Fill the reservoir; don't drain it dry."

Paul stood speechless at Dr. Vickerson's rapid-fire summarization of their day together.

"No, Paul, you don't have all afternoon," he continued. "You have an appointment over at the seminary library to start working on Sunday's sermon. If you can spend the next three hours working through the text for Sunday, studying several of the commentaries there, you'll be well on your way to saying something significant to your people. See you next week. 10:00 A.M. sharp!"

6

A Day
in the Life

By 5:00 P.M. Paul Andrews had completed his translation of Sunday's text and had studied several commentaries on the passage. He confined his study to commentaries that he didn't have back in his study, intending to read his own in the morning.

On the way home his mind reeled from his conversations with Dr. Vickerson. What struck him most was the need for pastors everywhere to get back to their real calling—prayer and the ministry of the Word. Dr. Vickerson had urged him before God to break out of his vicious circle of overcommitment to other areas. Loss of focus on his calling had resulted in the gradual slide into shoddy sermon preparation and poor preaching.

The subtle temptation was to think that since those other areas were important and good things, he should do them. But while they were necessary, other people in the church should be doing them, not the pastor. It was wrong for those things to take time away from his primary calling.

"How ironic," Paul thought. "The more important and needed I feel, the less I find myself carrying out my proper calling before God. All those 'indispensables' have piled up on me to the point of actually threatening my opportunity to stay with the church I now pastor. By being busy in too many areas I've jeopardized my usefulness in the one main area to which I've been called by God."

Paul knew he had to start thinking of prayer and the ministry of the Word as his *whole* business, his *one* business. He had discovered through firsthand experience that Beecher was right when he said no preacher was big enough to do more than preach.

He also thought how this lack of preparation and devotion to preaching the Word had contributed to the weakening of the church. Sheep were not being nurtured and fed the way they needed to be, and many were suffering from spiritual malnutrition.

In his imagination Paul pictured a flock of undernourished and diseased sheep, some too weak to stand, bleating pathetically for the shepherd to "do something about it."

Paul thought out loud as the scene flashed through his mind: "I will do something about it. By God's grace I will!"

Then he thought of the larger church. If he had fallen into the trap of uninspired and uninspiring preaching, how many hundreds, even thousands, of other preachers had done the same? How many others had also undervalued the preaching of the Word and misplaced their priorities, committing themselves to a thousand other tasks while neglecting the one business to which God had called them?

He pictured not only his own small flock of sheep, but the thousands of flocks represented by these preachers throughout the world, even down through church history. He saw a massive number, "a myriad too great to count," all bleating, stumbling, panting, weak, and unhealthy, begging to be fed. He remembered that somewhere in the Old Testament God had spoken of a famine for His Word. Indeed there was a famine.

The sheep in his imagination were more crippled and distressed than old Dr. Vickerson, arthritis and all. His was a physical problem, but theirs was spiritual. The vision disturbed him so greatly that he found himself weeping before God as his car sped down the parkway.

> *Paul thought about how his lack of preparation and devotion to preaching the Word had contributed to the weakening of the church. "I will do something about it. By God's grace I will!"*

Alone in his car, yet knowing he was not alone at all, Paul made a vow before the Lord, speaking aloud, almost in a shout:

> I, Paul Andrews, minister of the Lord Jesus Christ, dedicate myself anew to my high calling, to preach the Word of God with freshness and vitality, to feed and nurture my congregation with sermons of substance and power.

Nearing home, he slowed to take the exit ramp. As he stopped at the red light off the ramp he reflected on the positive effect that his early start had on Sunday's sermon. Already he was beginning to harness that tension and energy that Dr. Vickerson had diagramed. He toyed with different ways he could arrange the ideas he had gathered in his studies at the seminary library.

More than that was the joy of knowing it was only Monday. Usually Paul hadn't gotten this far until much later in the week, but now the whole week lay ahead to prepare his message. For the first time in months he was actually excited about preaching!

Then came Tuesday. The events of the week were not earth-shattering, just frustrating. Paul arrived in the office the next morning before his secretary, intending to take advantage of the early-morning quiet and get a jump on the day.

But then he noticed the answering machine flashing the news that someone had called. In fact several messages were on the phone. The most disturbing message was that Tim Foster would be stopping by early, maybe around 9:00 A.M., because he "had a few things" he wanted to talk about.

Tim was unemployed, and not eager to find work. He did have some sort of business that he operated, but he only worked when the spirit moved him. It seemed that the angel of the Lord seldom descended to "stir the waters." "Maybe only once each year, like in the Bible," Paul grumbled to himself. Tim would not have anything important to say, but he would have all the time in the world to say it.

Paul moaned to himself as he hastily drew a sketch of Tuesday's time-chart. He measured off the four columns for the time, the activity, the things that he should do, and the things others could be doing. He began the log at 7:45 A.M. His first entry was "Made time chart!"

"Aha!" he exclaimed as he filled in the columns. "I can get the secretary to prepare me a master sheet and duplicate it for each day. I'll need 13 more copies."

Paul was delighting in his small timesaving discovery when the phone rang. It was his secretary, Arlene. She had forgotten about her doctor's appointment this morning. She also had a family reunion coming up and wondered if she could take the whole day off to do some shopping for it.

Paul assured her there was no problem, then hung up the phone. "No problem for you, Arlene—just for me." Thoughts of answering all the phone calls unscreened did not inspire him. He entered "8:00—8:10 A.M."; "Phone call with Arlene." He paused at the column "I Should Do" and muttered to himself, "Well, I could have my secretary take the call, but the call came from my secretary."

Then the tape-recorder popped into his mind. He had decided to start taping his sermons again. At least he could listen to them to see if there was any improvement. Dr. Vickerson also had indicated that he would like to hear some sermon tapes later on.

He jumped from his seat and began searching the church classrooms for the recorder. Naturally, it wasn't until he tried the last place possible that he found it in the third-grade Sunday school room.

"One of Murphy's laws at work," he muttered to himself.

Then began the search for cassette tapes. Finding none, he wrote himself a note to pick up the blanks at lunchtime.

Finally Paul settled back in his seat, commentary in hand, and began to study. It was 8:30 now. He thought he would get in a good half-hour before Tim came. Tim came 20 minutes early.

It always amazed Paul how a man with nothing to do needed so much time to do it. He ambled into the office and plopped himself down in the seat across from Paul. He leaned back and relaxed, then with a big, contented smile said, "Well, how's it going these days, Pastor? Been keeping yourself busy lately?"

It was 11:15 when Tim finally left. He hinted about going to lunch, but Paul had another appointment (he didn't tell Tim it was an appointment to buy tapes). Their conversation had included a wide range of topics, from "Pastor, did you read in the paper this morning about that oil spill down in Texas?" to "I think I know how you can solve that problem with the neighborhood children riding their bicycles out in the parking lot during morning worship service."

Just then Mrs. McCracken burst into the office and took the seat Tim had vacated. She threw down some pattern books and a swatch of material onto his desk and began talking.

"Pastor, I know you're a busy man, but I didn't appreciate you canceling our appointment yesterday. We're anxious to get the drapes ordered so they can be installed before the end of summer. Your wife called to tell me you couldn't be here. Was it anything important? I hope so, because this matter is extremely important. We've been working on it for several months now."

"Good morning, Mrs. McCracken. Didn't you see me?" Tim was still standing in the doorway.

"Oh, I'm sorry Tim, I have so much on my mind. Now, Pastor Andrews, tell me what you think of this material. I showed it to all the ladies yesterday morning. This is the cloth they picked out. We're anxious to know your opinion. That's why I was so disappointed when you canceled our appointment. I had planned to head right over to place the order as soon as I left here. I do hope you had an important reason for canceling, Pastor." Mrs. McCracken was fishing and scolding at the same time.

Refusing to bite, Paul thought sarcastically to himself, "No, nothing important—just the spiritual welfare of the children of God. Nothing nearly as important as the drapes in the lounge of the church building."

Meanwhile Tim Foster, who had been lingering near the office door, watching, caught a nasty glance from Mrs. McCracken. Taking the hint, he slowly backed away and took his usual eternity to finally exit the church building.

"Mrs. McCracken, whatever the women have decided on, that is just fine with me."

"You do think the material is pretty, don't you?"

"Yes, but I'm not much good in helping with draperies. I would have to see the whole effect in the room before I could really appreciate it. I trust your judgment, Mrs. McCracken. Go ahead and order those drapes." He knew those last words were the words she wanted to hear.

Just then another member of the women's group arrived. Mrs. McCracken had been expecting her. They had arranged between themselves to meet with Paul to get his approval, then drive over together to place the order at the furniture store. Paul thought about how everyone seemed to schedule his appointments for him without ever consulting him first. He made a mental note of one of the changes that needed to take place if he was to make the time for pursuing his high calling.

Upon seeing Mrs. Shanor arrive, Mrs. McCracken jumped up from the seat. "He likes it!" she stated. "Pastor Andrews agrees with our choice of materials. He just now gave us the approval to go ahead and order the drapes! I told you he would like this material best, Hilda."

She grabbed Mrs. Shanor by the arm and rushed her out of the office. Hilda Shanor had just enough time to lean her head back into the doorway. "Hello, Pastor. Thanks for approving the drapes." Then she disappeared as Mrs. McCracken whisked her away to the furniture store.

Paul noted the time in his log: "11:55." Under "activity" he wrote "Lunch/buy tapes." The morning was gone. His afternoon would be devoted to hospital visitation. He would spend his evening with his family.

The whole week seemed to go that way for Paul. Was it typical or atypical? He wondered what a typical week is supposed to be for a pastor. So despite his early start, Paul's sermon preparation stalled.

He found himself struggling over the message on Saturday night. This time he was more prepared than he had been for quite some time, but something didn't feel quite right about the outline, about the message. He couldn't put his finger on it, but he had run out of time. He had to preach the message as it stood.

Susan was more enthusiastic about it than Paul. She observed a little more spirit in his sermon and delivery on Sunday morning. It seemed better prepared to her, and she sensed that the congregation noticed the difference too.

Her words encouraged Paul, but he still felt dissatisfied. Perhaps Dr. Vickerson would be able to shed some light on it. Paul dreaded to hear what the problem might be, but he wanted to hear the truth no matter how painful. Critical analysis of his preaching was too much like going through surgery: Cutting to the heart of the message also cut to the heart of the messenger.

Paul did not anticipate one interesting effect that his taping would have: Word began to spread in the church that he was seeking another call. Some speculated that he was taping his messages for pulpit committees to hear, that he was working harder on his preaching because he wanted to impress another church.

7

Rifles and Shotguns

Dr. Vickerson peered over Paul's sermon outline with a careful eye, tilting his wire-rimmed glasses as he read.

"I can see why you were a little uncomfortable with this, Paul."

Out of the corner of his eye he noticed Paul stiffen in anticipation of the bad news. "Relax, son!" he laughed. "This is quite an improvement over last week. Judging by your outline this was a good message. Did anyone notice a difference in your preaching on Sunday?"

Paul loosened a little. "My wife did, and she's my most honest critic. It's usually a good sign when she compliments me. I also received a few positive comments at the door."

"That's great! You have a good message here, son."

"I'm anxious to hear what it was that made me feel uncomfortable about it," Paul prodded.

"As your sermon now stands it lacks a clear dominating purpose. It actually contains three or four different ideas that are somewhat related, but not quite the same. Each one is strong enough to stand on its own as a message in itself."

"No wonder my poor congregation is tired of my preaching. They have to listen to three or four messages at once."

"The congregation probably didn't even notice what I'm saying. They were able to get good meat from your message. You didn't send them away hungry."

"I think I understand what you're saying, Dr. Vickerson. I found so many good points last Monday as I worked on the passage in the library that I guess I tried to force them all into one message."

"Sounds to me like some of that old enthusiasm to communicate the Word is coming back already, Paul."

"Why is it that as soon as you pointed out the problem I could see it immediately, but when I was home working on it I couldn't see it for the life of me?"

"For one thing, waiting until Saturday night gave you no time to resolve it. The mind often works on its own if you give it enough resting time. Another idea is to find a preacher who you consider above average and arrange to call each other for help whenever you get stumped like that."

"I don't think a call at 1:00 A.M. on Saturday night would be appreciated," Paul remarked as he thought back to last weekend.

Dr. Vickerson laughed "No, either way you need to give yourself more time to work on the message. Saturday night is too late."

"What should I do now, Dr. Vickerson? I started my series on Jonah last Sunday. Should I go back to Jonah 1 and try again or move on to Jonah 2?"

"You might save this outline and bring it out in a few years to use it again. But then divide it into three parts. Your messages will be much more directed, more powerful. Remember, you can say more about less. As the sermon stands now it's more like a shotgun than a rifle. You're shooting in several directions instead of taking careful aim at one target."

Dr. Vickerson laid Paul's outline back down on the table and reached for his little notebook. He searched its first few pages until he found what he wanted.

"Listen to this quote from Henry Ward Beecher, Paul":

> The sermon is not like a Chinese firecracker
> to be fired off for the noise it makes. It is a
> hunter's gun, and at every discharge he should
> look to see his game fall.

He read the quote a second time, more deliberately, with emphasis on the hunter's gun. Then he gently closed the worn booklet and set it back down.

"What Beecher is saying is that the sermon should have a clear purpose, a target. Like the rifle, it should be aimed carefully at that target to hit the mark."

"I guess that's what made me so uncomfortable with my sermon. I didn't quite know where it was going, what I was trying to accomplish by it."

"Yes, your intuition that something was amiss was correct. Before we forget, though, there is another important aspect about purpose that I want to stress. Paul, have you heard any 'word-association' sermons lately?"

"I'm familiar with word-association games, but I'm not sure what you mean by 'word-association' sermons," Paul replied with a puzzled look.

"They are sermons that are built around a key word in a passage of Scripture, while having little or no relation to the passage itself."

Paul still looked puzzled.

"Let me give you an example. Years ago while Emily and I were on vacation we stopped to worship at one of those large, well-known churches that young ministers dream of one day pastoring. Let me give you a sample of the sermon we heard to show you what I mean. It has been awhile, but I can still remember most of it."

Dr. Vickerson arose slowly from his kitchen table. He steadied himself, then struck a pose as if he were standing at an imaginary pulpit. He pasted on a warm, patronizing smile and looked out over his imaginary congregation. Then he began:

God so loved the world that He gave His only begotten Son (pause). God so loved that He gave (pause again). God gave (a third pause).

God gave. You should give too. God gave us His very best. His Son. His only begotten Son. We all need to give back to God. We need to give more to God than we ever have before.

This week marks our annual fund drive for the church budget. Teams of callers will be canvassing the church to solicit your pledge of support to the work of God. Remember, we serve a living God, a giving God. We must be a giving people.

Last year we fell short by 5 percent of our budget, but this year we want to reach our goal so the work can go on. Remember, God so loved that He gave. Do you love this church, this ministry?

I am reminded again of the little boy who didn't have much to give, but he gave what he could to Jesus. He had five loaves and two fishes. Do you remember that story? Remember how he gave all that he had and Jesus multiplied his gift? Remember how Jesus actually fed the 5000 with it? The little boy's gift was miraculously multiplied by God!

Give now so God may multiply your gifts and make miracles happen through you!

With that Dr. Vickerson stopped and slowly sat down.

Paul laughed at Dr. Vickerson's 'word-association' sermon. He had heard similar messages on tithing through the years.

"But the point I make, Paul, is not that it's a bad sermon on tithing. What the preacher did was use John 3:16 as a word-association game. He took off on the word 'gave' and never returned to the text. The purpose of that text is to communicate the message of the gospel—not our stewardship, but our need for a Savior."

"The apostle Paul does use the sacrifice of Christ as a motivation for stewardship," Paul countered. "After all, he said, 'Thanks be to God for His unspeakable gift.'"

"Yes, and the sacrifice of Christ is the greatest motivation for stewardship. But this message totally misses the purpose of John 3:16. Remember why John told us he wrote this book?

> ... these have been written that you may believe that Jesus is the Christ, the Son of God, and that believing you may have life in His name (John 20:31).

"That is its governing purpose. That is the meaning behind John 3:16. How many tithing sermons have been taken from this passage and given in churches where the gospel itself is not clearly preached!"

"'Word-association' preaching," Paul summarized as he wrote in his notebook, "means using a key word from the text to take off on a tangent not necessarily related to the purpose of the text itself."

"It's pathetic, Paul. Preachers will talk for 20 or 30 minutes on everything but their text. They dare to stand as God's representatives without backing their words with His Word. It's also dangerous! Imagine what it will be like to stand before the judgment throne of God having played so footloose with His Word!"

"Was my sermon guilty of this?" Paul asked sheepishly.

"Not at all; you stuck closely to the Scriptures. That's why I keep telling you your message was a good one. But word-association preaching has at least three major faults to it. First, by straying so far from the text, the preacher invites theological error. Second, that kind of preaching teaches the congregation to study their Bibles the same way. No wonder people come up with so many bizarre interpretations of the will of God for their lives! They use Scripture the same way they hear their pastors using it. Third, since the sermon never really matches the purpose of the text, the listener might conclude that the Bible is irrelevant to life. The preacher has only used it as a springboard for his own ideas."

"And that might encourage people to stop reading their Bibles altogether," Paul added.

"Exactly. Either they read with a license to play the same word-association games that their preacher plays, or they conclude that there's no good reason to read Scripture at all."

Then as he seemed fond of doing, Dr. Vickerson quickly changed the tone and heaviness of the conversation. "I'm ready for one of those sandwiches now, Paul."

Susan had packed some tunafish sandwiches for the two men. She had also made a fresh batch of brownies topped with thick chocolate icing. To go with the sandwiches she sent along a fresh fruit cup of sliced strawberries and bananas, plus apples, grapes, and oranges.

"Susan apologizes for the tuna sandwiches, and she says she intends to make up for them by inviting you to our home for dinner sometime. We both remember those wonderful feasts your wife prepared for the students back in seminary."

"She doesn't need to apologize for the tunafish, Paul. It is a favorite of mine, and I can't wait to bite into one of those brownies."

Paul gave the blessing and a short period of silence followed as the two attacked their sandwiches. Then between mouthfuls Dr. Vickerson returned to his teaching. "Paul, your sermon should always be formulated into a purpose statement. You remember that, of course, from seminary."

"I remember but I often forget to actually do it."

"I'm afraid you aren't the only preacher who forgets, but it's essential. That purpose statement should be clearly worded, and it should agree with the purpose the Holy Spirit had in mind when He inspired the writer of that text."

"Don't you think it presumptuous to read the Holy Spirit's mind?" Paul couldn't help but ask.

"Not at all. Isn't that the goal of careful exegesis— studying the text in its larger context? Comparing it with cross-references and parallel passages? Gleaning from various commentaries and study books? That is why it's called *exegesis* and not *eisegesis*. Your purpose is to discover God's purpose in it! No, Paul, it is *not* presumptuous to try to find out what God means when He inspires a passage. How else can the preacher 'speak as it were the utterances of God,' as 1 Peter 4:11 commands you to?"

As Paul wrote, he indicated to Dr. Vickerson that he was convinced.

"That purpose statement puts a target before your sermon. Your whole message should be structured to hit the bull's-eye. Remember to use your rifle, not your shotgun! To put it another way, the purpose is your *destination*, and the sermon structure is the *vehicle* you will use to reach that destination."

Paul sensed the value of Dr. Vickerson's last statement. He put down the brownie he had just picked up and reached for his notebook again. "Could you repeat that last statement again, sir? I want to be sure to get it right."

"Gladly. *The purpose statement is your sermon's destination. The sermon structure you choose is your vehicle to reach it.*"

Paul finished writing and started to trade his pen for that brownie when Dr. Vickerson interrupted him again.

"While you still have that pen in your hand, write down another word in your notes. The word is *aphorism*. If you want your congregation to hear the purpose of the sermon in a way they won't miss, shape that statement into an aphorism."

Paul gave a blank look as he dutifully wrote the word "aphorism" in his notes.

"Jesus loved to teach that way. In fact, someone has taken the time to count all the aphorisms of Christ in the four Gospels. Let me see, I have that number here somewhere."

Paul watched as the old professor's bent fingers fumbled through his notebook to find the place.

"Yes, here it is: 133 separate aphorisms in the four Gospels, and 368 when you add the repeats in the parallel accounts! When you consider how many verses of the Gospel accounts are given to narrative or have people other than Christ speaking, that number is even more amazing. Almost everything Jesus said, He says in aphoristic form!"

Paul wrote down the numbers but remained perplexed. Dr. Vickerson seemed too caught up in his own enthusiasm over the subject to notice.

"So turn your purpose statements into aphorisms, Paul! If Jesus, the Master Communicator—the Word made flesh—used them, we servants are not above our Master."

Ordinarily Paul would admit his ignorance, but today there had already been too much to admit; his ego would have a hard time handling much more. So he smiled and nodded, then said firmly, "I sure will, Dr. Vickerson. I'll work on that for my next sermon." Secretly he thought, "I have no idea what an aphorism is!"

8

Preaching with Aphorisms

That afternoon Paul began his studies in the library by thumbing through the "A" section of his dictionary. When he found what he was looking for he stopped and read:

> Aphorism: a short, pointed sentence expressing a truth or precept; maxim, adage.

Paul pondered the definition for awhile, then searched to see if the library had anything on the aphorisms of Christ.

Dr. Vickerson's remarks about Jesus employing aphorisms had aroused his curiosity. Not only that, but Paul had also promised to "work on that" for his next sermon.

The new librarian was able to point him to the back of a reference work containing a list of the aphorisms of Christ and a chart showing which were repeated in the various Gospel accounts. The listed included sayings such as:

- What does it profit a man if he gain the whole world and lose his own soul?
- No man can serve two masters; for either he will hate the one and love the other, or he will hold to the one and despise the other.
- Ask and it shall be given you; seek and you shall find; knock and it shall be opened to you.

As Paul examined the chart it began to dawn on him how heavily Jesus relied on the power of aphorisms.

Glancing over at the librarian he mumbled under his breath, "She's not so bad after all." On cue she looked up at him from her desk as if she heard him. He gave her a silly smile, then hurried back to his desk.

There he made some appropriate notes on the subject. He discovered that the word "aphorism" was derived from the Greek *aphorizo,* meaning "to separate, to set apart." From it came the English "horizon," that place in the distance that sets apart earth from sky.

Jesus used an aphorism to accent a particular truth and set it apart in memorable form. Even if the crowd or the disciples didn't immediately grasp what He was saying, they would remember His words long after He had spoken them.

Paul read through the Sermon on the Mount and found almost every statement shaped this way. No wonder the sayings of Jesus were so powerful, finding their way even into the secular speech of a world that had all but forgotten the Lord—sayings like "the blind leading the blind," "turning the other cheek," and "ask and it shall be given to you."

As he turned to the exegesis and study of Jonah, Paul grew excited about shaping his purpose statement into an aphorism for Sunday's sermon.

Jesus accented particular truths and set them apart in memorable form. Even if the crowd or the disciples didn't immediately grasp what He was saying, they would remember His words long after He had spoken them.

He read back over the first chapter of Jonah, comparing it with his sermon outline from the day before. He could clearly see now how his first sermon covering all of Jonah 1 had the potential for three or four sermons instead of one.

"Why should I wait several years to preach again on this passage?" Paul thought to himself. "Why not go back to chapter 1 and do it now?"

He had spent considerable time on the background of the book, giving appropriate introductory remarks the week before. He had also emphasized Jonah's flight from the Lord and how the ship he boarded was headed in the opposite direction from God's commission.

"There's one sermon on running away from God's commands," Paul thought. "I could have stopped at the end of verse 3 yesterday, but I covered it well enough that I better go on to verse 4 and begin there for this Sunday."

As he restudied the passage Paul suddenly realized that he had done most of his homework the previous week. Now he could concentrate more on creatively dealing with the materials before him. Waiting for weekends to prepare his messages left little time for imaginative or creative work. Nor did it leave much opportunity for thinking carefully about the application of the text. Besides, spending several intense hours in study always left his brain too fatigued for those aspects of sermon preparation. Dr. Vickerson's insistence upon starting early gave him opportunity to rest, then come back fresh to the work.

As Paul read over the next few verses of Jonah 1 he began to see his sermon emerge from the text.

"Jonah was sleeping below deck while above the sailors were fighting for their lives," Paul spoke in a loud whisper. Dr. Vickerson had always emphasized writing sermons for the ear to hear rather than the eye to read. By talking aloud Paul could think of how his words would sound to his congregation. The library was empty, so he felt safe about talking to himself.

"Jonah asleep, the sailors afraid . . . Jonah sleeping, the sailors praying to their gods. Praying to their gods! That's it!" Paul exclaimed. "The believer is sleeping while the world is praying! What a strange effect our disobedience has on the planet! It reverses everything."

Paul read on to verse 6. The captain, finding Jonah, shakes him and asks, "How is it that you are sleeping? Get up, call on your god. Perhaps your god will be concerned about us so that we will not perish."

"The world is telling the believer to pray," Paul continued talking to himself. He wrote hastily as thoughts poured forth: "The world telling the believer to wake up and pray! That is often what happens when the world faces a disaster. An unbeliever's child gets deathly sick so she runs to the believer next door to ask for prayer for the child. Perhaps the believer had tried to witness to her before, only to be cut short. But when the storms of life strike, the believer's door is the first door the world knocks on."

"That's not so unusual, but what *is* unusual is that the believer is sleeping while the world is praying," Paul continued to think out loud. "But is that unusual? Maybe not. Maybe a lot of us are sleeping, right here in this congregation, while the world around us is crying out in the storm."

Paul saw a powerful message emerging. His mind was

filled with exciting possibilities. He also began contemplating his own particular audience. This brought an often-missing dimension to his message, a dimension that a late start in sermon preparation could seldom offer.

"To what in our world are we blind because we're sleeping? Jonah was so trapped in his own rebellion that he curled up in depression and fell asleep. He lost all concern for the world abovedeck. In what ways are we like Jonah?" Paul put down his pen and sat back to ponder.

Suddenly he caught a glimpse of the clock at the opposite end of the reference room. He had been so engrossed in his work that he didn't realize his time was gone.

"What a difference from that feeling of drudgery on a Saturday night!" He said as he rose from his seat.

"Are you talking to me?" the librarian asked quizzically. She had suddenly appeared in the room as Paul spoke these last words. Her break into Paul's deep thoughts both startled and embarrassed him.

"No, just to myself," he managed to say as he quickly picked up his belongings and stumbled in the direction of the security device.

9

Jonah Snoring

That evening when Susan and the two boys rode with Paul after supper to the nearby ice cream stand, the boys in the back seat were in lively form. (Paul had warned Susan that naming them James and John, "the sons of thunder," was a big mistake.) However, this night their conversation was more humor than thunder.

John related an incident from Sunday school class the day before. A bee had flown into the room through an open window and was buzzing around the room, causing all the children some anxious moments—all this during the middle of the lesson.

The only two who didn't notice the bee were Miss Clayton and Mary Elizabeth. They were deeply involved in a conversation with each other about some Bible character.

"What was your lesson about, John?" Susan interrupted John's account.

"Oh, I forget, mom. We were all too worried about this bee. It was going bzzzzz, bzzzzz all over the room." John imitated the bee's buzzing. Then gesturing with his hands he continued, "Everyone's pointing at it and ducking and whispering to each other 'Look out! It's a bee!' Meanwhile Mary Elizabeth keeps raising her hand and waving it to answer Miss Clayton. She's always flapping her hand in the air to show off."

"Be kind, John." It was Paul's turn to interrupt.

"Just then that bee lands right on top of her shiny black shoe. And it starts crawling up her sock!"

"She didn't even see it?" James asked in amazement.

"No! She never saw it! She just kept on talking to Miss Clayton," John replied. "Then the bee climbed up to her bare leg. Mary Elizabeth stopped waving her hand and reached down to scratch her leg."

"Did it sting her?" James shrieked.

"Let me finish, James!"

"Boys," Paul and Susan chimed in together.

"When she touched the bee it just went BZZZZZZZ and started to fly away, BUT IT GOT CAUGHT UNDER HER DRESS!" John was now shouting the gory details.

"What happened? What happened?" James could hardly wait.

"Mary Elizabeth screamed her lungs out. She jumped out of her seat and fell backward over her chair. Then she grabbed her dress and pulled it up high and started kicking her feet into the air like crazy. The whole time she keeps yelling , 'NO! NO! NO! GET OUT OF HERE, BEE! GET OUT! IS IT OUT YET? DID IT GET OUT?' "

The way John related the story had everyone laughing so hard that tears were rolling down their faces as they pulled into the ice cream stand parking lot.

"What happened next? Did you kill the bee?" James asked.

"Finally the bee buzzed out from under her dress and flew out the window."

"The poor little girl! Did she get hurt, John?" Susan asked while trying to contain her laughter.

"Nah, she was okay, mom. She was just all upset and crying, so Miss Clayton took her out to the water fountain to calm her down."

"The old fountain trick works every time," Paul chuckled.

Then John added, "That's why I don't remember the lesson, mom."

That evening Paul thought again about the honeybee incident as he and Susan were preparing for bed. "Children are so expressive," he said. "They put so much excitement and enthusiasm into their words. Even with their limited vocabularies they can paint such vivid pictures. They throw their whole bodies into their descriptions."

"Somewhere we lose all that as we grow up. Our speech is so dull and lifeless compared to theirs," Susan remarked. Then she half-jokingly added as she reached for the light switch, "Maybe you preachers ought to listen more to how children talk. You might learn something about that freshness you're looking for."

"What if we tried to preach more the way children talk?" Paul continued thinking to himself as Susan drifted off to sleep.

Preaching had become the center of his attention these days. No matter what was happening throughout the day, Paul kept relating it back to preaching. It was just as Dr. Vickerson had said earlier when he spoke of streams flowing into the pulpit instead of flowing away from it. Preaching was rapidly becoming Paul's "one business."

"Children use so much expression. They add all kinds of crazy sound effects to demonstrate what they mean— bees buzzing, desks and chairs screeching across the floor while poor Mary Elizabeth jumps up to get the bee out from under her dress. Such sound effects. John is pretty good at them."

Suddenly Susan, lying beside him, broke into a loud snore, the kind that happened occasionally just as she fell into a deeper sleep.

"Snoring," Paul thought. "What a sound effect that is, snoring."

"Snoring!" he thought again as he sat up in bed. "Jonah snoring in the boat! What if I have Jonah do some actual snoring in my sermon on Sunday! I think I like that idea! I think Jonah will snore for us this Sunday!"

10

Shaping the Purpose into an Aphorism

"So they liked your snoring," Dr. Vickerson laughed.

"For once on a Sunday the preacher was asleep while the congregation was awake," Paul replied.

"No, Paul, not for once. The way your preaching is improving your people won't be sleeping very often. This sermon on Jonah sounds quite effective."

Dr. Vickerson's remarks were kind and edifying, and Paul felt like running out to get started on next week's sermon. Somewhere deep inside the flame for preaching was being rekindled. Confidence was returning.

"Listen closely to good public speakers, Paul. You'll be surprised at how often they make sounds and noises like your snoring. Smart communicators know when to use nondictionary sounds effectively. In fact, they're so good at it that you don't hear the technique at all, but just an enhanced message."

"I must admit, I was hesitant to snore in my sermon. I felt a little uneasy about it."

"With practice it will become more natural. In fact, you'll start hearing when speakers don't include it, and it will sound unnatural to you. You'll sense the thought begging for an appropriate descriptive noise!

"Now let's take a closer look at your sermon on Jonah."

"I'm not sure whether my sermon's purpose statement, or 'destination,' as you call it, is written as an aphorism."

"So you did some study on aphorisms?" Dr. Vickerson lowered his glasses and gave a knowing look.

Paul blushed. "Why, Dr. Vickerson, I've known all about aphorisms for a long time now—at least a week! An aphorism is 'a short, pointed sentence expressing a truth or precept; maxim, adage.' "

As they both laughed Paul's momentary embarrassment was overcome by his growing admiration and love for his mentor.

"I wish every preacher I know could have the privilege of your counsel, Dr. Vickerson."

"Son, you wouldn't want to do that to the church of Jesus Christ. It has enough troubles already. Besides, not every preacher has your heart for improvement. Remember, the first principle of preaching with freshness is *determination*. It takes a willingness to be different, to work hard at it, to make it your ministry's highest priority. No, I'm afraid there are too few like yourself who see the importance of preaching. Let the laypeople do all those needed ministries and the preachers do the preaching!

"When Jesus Christ ascended on high He gave gifts to His church," Dr. Vickerson continued. "One of His greatest gifts was preachers and teachers, who are listed right next to apostles, prophets, and evangelists. That's what Ephesians 4 tells us."

"So as a preacher I'm God's gift to the church?" Paul's question carried a hint of sarcasm.

"Think of it! God gives gifts to the church. In this special list is 'preachers and teachers.' Yet those entrusted with the sacred gifts necessary for inspiring, for exhorting, for training and edifying the congregation become inoperative. They do things like type bulletins, chair committee after committee, sit around at ministerial meetings, and. . . ."

". . . and help pick out the drapes for the lady's lounge," Paul continued. "And listen for hours to people like Tim Foster talk about the problems of the world while never doing anything about them."

"One of Satan's favorite tactics is to keep preachers busy with 'church work' instead of being about their Father's business. We need to learn to refuse to do the many good ministries in order to properly do the one right ministry."

"Do you think this is one reason for much of the church's anemic and weak condition?"

Dr. Vickerson shook his head sadly. "Shallow and shoddy preaching has seriously harmed Christianity. That has to be one reason so many immature believers are desperate for counseling all the time. If they only knew God's Word and were being motivated each week by strong, inspiring preaching they wouldn't get themselves into so many messy situations."

"So we preachers need to return to our true calling from the Lord," Paul summarized.

"Paul, it reminds me of children at Christmas playing with the boxes and wrapping paper instead of their expensive toys. Somewhere buried under all the wrappings and clutter of 'ministry' is that priceless, God-given gift of preaching."

"Whose fault is it—the preacher's or the congregation's?"

"It's both, of course, but the preacher must be the catalyst for change by making the Church Board and congregation aware of it. It takes education as well as a determination to stick to your high calling when well-meaning members try to burden you with wrong expectations."

"I think I've fallen into the trap of trying to please everyone in the church. It seems like every member is my boss, when my real boss should be the Lord."

"But you're determined to do something about it!" Dr. Vickerson smiled. "Keep working this week on that time study and maybe we'll be ready to deal with these matters by next time."

"Back to the subject of aphorisms, Dr. Vickerson. It seems a little hard to come up with ways of shaping the sermon's purpose into an aphorism. Don't you think it requires more creativity than most preachers have? I realize that Jesus preached that way, but how many of us can preach like Jesus?"

"None of us can ever fully measure up to His standard, but He still commands us to reach for it. True, it takes some extra effort to work aphorisms into the sermon, but most preachers don't even try to make the effort."

"Many of us have probably never even thought of making that a part of sermon preparation," Paul responded.

"But the world tries to make the effort, Paul. Open your ears and listen. The advertising world works hard to find catchy slogans and sayings that stick in the consumer's mind long after the commercial is over."

"Do you consider those aphorisms?" Paul asked, confident of his dictionary knowledge of the word.

"Many are not, but some are. But the principle is similar: Statements are worded in a catchy way. Even if they have no substance, the advertiser wants the customer to believe they contain great wisdom.

"Perhaps an even better place to listen is in the music industry," Dr. Vickerson continued. "A common practice in music is to build the song around an aphorism. The refrain usually contains the saying, while the verses build on it."

"Can you give me an example?"

"I have an excellent example for you, Paul. I'll even grant you permission to use it in a sermon sometime if you like. I once heard a song on the radio that kept repeating the theme 'I wonder how the other half die.' As I heard it I immediately thought of the apostle Paul's statement 'For to me to live is Christ and to die is gain.' "

"I never thought of it before, but what an aphorism that statement is! That's one of my favorite verses in the Bible," Paul interrupted.

"One of mine, too. But contrast that to the statement in the song 'I wonder how the other half die.' Just how *do* the 'other half' die? Those without Christ? Those without the assurance that 'to die is gain'? I think that would make for a very challenging sermon on sharing our faith with the lost."

"I see what you mean. I wish you would have told me this before yesterday's sermon. While Jonah was snoring the other half were facing death—and not very well at that!"

"You may still be able to work the idea into a later sermon from the book of Jonah, Paul. But there's one other thing I want to say before I forget it: The songwriter took a familiar saying about the 'other half' and gave it a slight twist. Instead of 'I wonder how the other half live,' the writer wondered how they die. That's the reason the song caught my attention as it did. A worn-out cliché was made fresh by that one modification."

"I remember back when I was a child," Paul recalled. "Our minister was fond of repeating the saying 'You've got to take the bad with the good.' He said it so often that we began to make a game of guessing each Sunday if he would repeat it or not. If he did, we could hardly keep from giggling out loud in our seats."

"I wish I had a nickel for every time my mother told me, 'You reap what you sow, young man,' " Dr. Vickerson laughed. "She said it each time she brought out the wooden spoon to discipline me. But you see the point of it, Paul. The reason those old clichés have become so tired and worn is that they summarize truth in a short, pithy form.

Your concern is to make sure you don't dull your congregation by repeating something the same way they've heard it a hundred times before. So one way to create an aphorism is to borrow an old one and add a new twist to it."

"Wouldn't the same be true for catchphrases and theological jargon, Dr. Vickerson?"

"An excellent observation, and we'll talk more about words and phrases at some future session. Right now I could go for some ice-cold lemonade. Could you get the pitcher out of the refrigerator for us, Paul? Then between now and lunch we can talk about those vehicles I spoke of last week."

Shallow and shoddy preaching is one reason so many immature believers are desperate for counseling. If they were being motivated each week by strong, inspiring preaching they wouldn't get into so many messy situations.

11

Vary the Vehicles

"Let's talk about vehicles, ways for your sermon's purpose to reach its destination," Dr. Vickerson said as he put down his glass of lemonade.

"When I was stuck in that rut of last-minute preparation," Paul confessed, "I hardly had time to jot down some notes on the passage, let alone think of creative ways to outline my message."

"By starting early you allow time to work on sermon structure. Remember, your purpose statement is your sermon's destination, its 'chief end,' to borrow a phrase from theology. Your outline becomes the vehicle to drive that message to its destination."

"What are the various types of outlines I can use?"

"There are many kinds of structures. It's good to change your approach from time to time to hold your people's interest—and your own, too. How you order your sermon can make a great difference as to how effective it is.

"You need to attack this part of your preparation after you have rested from all that tedious exegesis of the passage. Your mind must be fresh if your sermon is to be fresh.

"First arrange your key ideas in a neat and readable form. Then begin to wrestle with those materials the way Jacob wrestled with the angel. Say to your notes before you, 'I won't let you go until you give me a blessing!'"

The professor paused for another drink of lemonade, then turned to a section in his little notebook.

He read from W. E. Sangster:

> The man whose architecture is splendidly varied has the people curious before the foundation is in. They hear the text and they ask themselves at once, "How will he build on that?"

"Do you see the effect that variety has on a congregation, Paul? If you keep from using the same routine every time, your people will be curious to see how you deal with the passage before you even start. Your reputation for delightful variety will fuel their expectations from week to week."

There are many kinds of structures. It's good to change your approach from time to time to hold your people's interest— and your own, too.

"Is there a list somewhere of types of sermon structures I can use?" Paul asked.

"It might be good for us to compile our own list, Paul. Can you give me some right now?"

"There are the obvious ones—topical, textual, and expository preaching," Paul quickly stated.

"Yes, and you tend toward the expository style, Paul, giving a verse-by-verse exposition of what the passage is saying. There is a kind of natural variety in that approach because Scripture has variety in itself."

"Sometimes I feel like I squeeze all the variety and life out of the text by the time I'm done with it."

"Preachers have been guilty of reducing Scripture, with all its vitality, to a wooden list of doctrinal statements. Doctrine is important, but we should try to communicate it more the way God communicates it in His Word."

"What are some other ways to structure the sermon?" Paul was compiling a list with some brief explanatory notes.

"A very popular way of preaching these days is the narrative sermon," Dr. Vickerson continued. "Narrative preaching takes a great deal of effort and imagination, but if you do it well you will hold your congregation's interest. There is power in a story well told."

"I've avoided that approach because I felt I couldn't communicate a lot of substance that way. I like to give my people meat and not just milk. Doesn't narrative preaching sacrifice the meat?"

"On the surface it might seem to, but further reflection might prove otherwise. Remember that Jesus is the Word of God incarnate. As God He could overwhelm us with vast storehouses of wisdom spoken in deep technical terms, but He recognized human limitations when He addressed the masses."

"Calvin said it was like a father lisping with his children," Paul remembered hearing somewhere.

"A good way to put it. Jesus used stories all the time. He taught in parables, as you well know."

"I'll never forget my seminary coursework on the parables; it was one of my favorite classes."

"One reason it's a favorite is the popular appeal of stories," Dr. Vickerson continued, pressing his point. "Now, Paul, if Jesus knew the limitations of His audience and the power of the story to communicate, why don't His followers use His methods more often? Naturally He is the Master, but at least we should try."

"Don't you agree with me that you sacrifice substance with that approach?" Paul asked.

"Yes and no. Some sermons bombard people with so many truths that they're overwhelmed. Hearing so much, they remember so little. Wouldn't it be better to impress one important truth upon them, to bring it home with such power, that they're not likely to forget it? That's what a well-told story can do. Look at the very book you're preaching on right now, Paul. I consider Jonah one of the finest short stories in all of literature."

"Yes, I never cease to marvel at its power," Paul agreed.

"So, yes, you may not be able to communicate as many different doctrinal truths in a narrative sermon, but the truths you *do* communicate will stay longer with the people through the power of the story.

"But let's move on," Dr. Vickerson continued as he eyed the clock. "Closely related to narrative preaching is what Andrew Blackwood liked to call 'biographical preaching.' He wisely observed the power that the story of people's lives has on other people. Watch how closely your people listen when you trace a personality like Samson or doubting Thomas. They see themselves reflected in the lives of Bible characters."

"I preached once on Peter wavering after Pentecost in his hypocrisy over the Gentiles. I read from Galatians 2, where Paul opposed Peter face-to-face over his sin. The congregation responded well to it."

"That kind of sermon speaks powerfully to those who want to drop out of church because of inconsistency and sin in the body of Christ."

"Some were shocked to see that even an apostle can fall into sin and hypocrisy."

Dr. Vickerson quickly added, "The great advantage of narrative or biographical sermons, or any sermons that follow a historical arrangement of events, is how easy they are for the preacher to remember. The wind could blow your notes right off the pulpit and you wouldn't miss a beat."

"And that's not true of complicated doctrinal sermons," Paul observed.

"Yes, that's exactly the point, Paul. If you as the preacher need to follow the outline of your sermon closely in order to remember what you want to say, how can you expect your people to remember it?"

"You're right about that. Sometimes I even forget what I preached on the week before!"

"Even when you're not using the narrative format, you should still labor over your outline until it is simple and uncomplicated. The outline should recall itself to you as you go along. The less you, the preacher, must rely on your notes, the more your people are likely to remember what you say."

Dr. Vickerson slowly repeated his last remark as Paul wrote. Then he went on, "That may not *always* be the case, but it usually is. If you've been able to structure your message in a very uncomplicated form, one that is logical, reasonable, and easy to follow, then your congregation stands a better chance of remembering it. Your sermon has to say something important, and it has to say it well, but the outline is the vehicle by which you say it."

"Can you give me a few more examples of 'vehicles,' Dr. Vickerson?"

The old professor thought for a moment, drumming his bent fingers on the top of the table. "One of my favorites is what might be called a 'two-point antithesis' sermon. The Lord Jesus spoke this way when He contrasted light with darkness, the solid rock with the sinking sand, God with Mammon, the rich man with poor Lazarus.

"It is an easy sermon to illustrate with body language. When you speak of the kingdom of darkness you can gesture to your left. When you speak of the kingdom of light you can gesture to your right, giving the congregation a visual cue to help them follow your message. The contrasts between the two are easy to remember, and even if the congregation doesn't get every single point, they at least get the *main* point. And they won't forget it."

"Can you give me an example of a sermon using antithesis?"

"I remember one I used for communion contrasting the death of Judas with the death of Jesus. I called it 'Golgotha and Hakeldema.' At Golgotha Jesus died in isolation, buying for us eternal life with His Father. At Hakeldema Judas died in isolation, his 30 pieces of silver purchasing this field of blood. I simply went back and forth contrasting communion with God to isolation from God."

"It sounds like a powerful message for communion. Do you mind if I use the idea sometime?" Paul asked.

"You would flatter me if you did!" Dr. Vickerson laughed, then went on. "You can vary the antithetical sermon two ways. The first is by going back and forth contrasting the two ideas throughout the message. Or you can give all of the one side first, then contrast it with the other side during the second half of the sermon."

"An example of the second approach?"

"I tackled predestination once in a sermon entitled 'A Tale of Two Chapters.' In the first half of the sermon I outlined briefly all the wonderful promises of Romans 8. Then in the second half I introduced Romans 9, where it deals with Jacob and Esau and God hardening Pharaoh's heart."

"That sounds very interesting. I never heard of anyone covering two chapters of Romans in one sermon."

"I had already preached for several weeks on Romans 8, so I merely summarized in rapid succession all its glorious truths: There is no condemnation in Christ; nothing can separate us from the love of God in Christ Jesus; the Spirit intercedes within us, the Son intercedes at the right hand of the Father; etc."

"What about Romans 9?" Paul asked.

"I just introduced Romans 9 with the promise of look-ing more closely at it in future weeks. I made the transition between the two chapters by saying, 'That's Romans 8, but don't forget that after Romans 8 comes Romans 9. Jacob I loved, but Esau I hated. God will have mercy on whom He desires, and He will harden whom He desires. It is the same Bible, the same book, the same writer, inspired by the same Spirit. People, you cannot take Romans 8 unless you are willing to take Romans 9!' "

"It sounds like a powerful message," Paul said with admiration. "How did the people react to it?"

"How about if we talk about it over lunch? I've really been hungry for some good Chinese food lately. Do you like Chinese cooking, Paul?"

12

Persuasion and Procedure

Bright orange goldfish swam back and forth in the giant aquarium adjacent to the table where the professor and Paul were seated. On the aquarium floor a toy replica of a wrecked sailing vessel sent a steady stream of bubbles to the surface above.

As Paul stared momentarily at the fish tank his retired professor began again to discuss various ways to structure sermons. Now his emphasis centered on "persuasive" and "procedural" messages.

"Shouldn't every sermon persuade, Dr. Vickerson?" Paul turned his gaze from the tank to the professor.

"Yes, every sermon should persuade, but I'm thinking more now of preaching that proves and reasons by scriptural and logical deduction—the kind of preaching which Paul used on his missionary journeys. Remember how he entered the synagogues in each city to 'reason' and 'persuade' the people of Christ and His resurrection?

"Examples of persuasive preaching include arguing for doctrinal positions such as the trinity or the deity of Christ. Often persuasive preaching might deal with touchy matters, such as speaking in tongues or abortion. You need to be very sensitive to your audience when it comes to such emotional issues."

"I know some preachers who say you should never preach on a controversial issue from the pulpit. How do you respond to that?"

"Well, sometimes it's good for those kinds of issues to be discussed in a setting where there can be immediate response, questions, and concerns raised. But I'm afraid our pulpits are all too tame and safe—so tame and safe that we bore our congregations. I don't think a steady diet of controversy is good, but an occasional sermon on a hot issue is healthy if the congregation perceives that it has been handled fairly. Jesus didn't get crucified and Paul didn't get stoned or run out of town by preaching safe sermons. Besides, your people are probably anxious to hear God's Word on certain controversial issues. And you won't have to worry about anyone falling asleep!"

"Can you give me an example of how you might handle a hot issue from the pulpit?"

"Paul, you're always testing me for examples! But that's a sign of a good student: Leave nothing to theory. You tell me what some hot issue in your congregation might be, and let me think of an approach that is sensitive to your audience."

"That's easy. How about infant baptism? Our denomination practices infant baptism, but many of our people don't believe in it."

"Infant baptism," Dr. Vickerson repeated as he drummed the table with his crooked, bony fingers.

Almost on cue the waitress arrived with some steaming hot wonton soup and fresh egg rolls.

"Saved by the food!" Dr. Vickerson laughed. "Seriously, Paul, you need to think about your audience. Think about the attitudes of those who oppose infant baptism. What are some of the things you hear them saying? How do they react over the issue?"

"They usually think infant baptism is done out of tradition and superstition."

"Often they're right about that!" Dr. Vickerson exclaimed.

"And they don't think there is any biblical evidence for it."

"Scripture does seem to be silent on it. You have to admit, Paul, there is no command in the New Testament saying, 'Thou shalt baptize infants.' What else comes out in their attitudes?"

"One of the things I hear a lot is that we should be like Jesus. Jesus was baptized as an adult and He went 'down into the waters,' so we should do the same."

"Okay, so you have isolated some of the key attitudes and defenses of those who oppose infant baptism. It would be good to make up a list of the ideas we just mentioned, then try to shape your sermon in such a way as to anticipate and respond to those attitudes and objections."

"Dr. Vickerson, your egg roll is getting cold."

"Let me finish my thoughts before I get caught up in the revelry of this fine Chinese cooking. Your sermon must do several things in order to be successful. First, it should be kind and nondefensive. You need to be sure and secure in your conviction if you are to preach on this issue. You must be certain that your own stand on infant baptism is not rooted in tradition or superstition or denominational loyalty.

"Second, you want to win over those who oppose your position. You may not convince them in one message that infant baptism is right, but you must convince them that you are sensitive to their position and that you appreciate their concerns. They have challenged you in a good way to search the Scriptures, to make sure you are resting on the authority of God's Word and not on man-made traditions. You should begin by thanking them for that!

"I also thought of something else. You might want to include the idea of Reformation abuses over baptism. We are always bragging about the Reformation, but this is one area where some of the Reformers were excessive and extreme. People were actually put to death over the matter of baptism. One particular man by the name of Felix Manz was drowned by those who opposed his views on immersion. They would say, 'Let those who want to go under the water go under the water!'

"You might begin by saying, 'Isn't it wonderful that we can disagree as Christian brothers and sisters over the issue of baptism, yet sit side by side and worship our Lord together!' Then sincerely thank your Baptist friends for their challenge that has led you back to the Scriptures to search for biblical answers to the issue of baptism.

"The other thing that is so important to stress is to firmly root your sermon in Scripture. I would try to keep all my arguments totally within the bounds of Scripture, without a single appeal to tradition. You want to remove any appearance of some extrabiblical authority determining your position and practice."

"I know that whenever I've had an opportunity to present the biblical case for infant baptism," Paul interrupted, "many have expressed surprise. They had never heard a biblical case before. But what about the charge of superstition?"

"Let me swallow this mouthful of egg roll and I'll try to answer you."

"I'm sorry. Take your time and enjoy your food while it's still hot."

"There," Dr. Vickerson gulped. "When it comes to superstition, you need to admit openly that there are those who baptize their children out of superstition. Then emphasize that abuses of truth do not change the truth. For example, some abuse the doctrine of salvation by grace, turning it into a license to sin. But that doesn't change the truth of the doctrine itself. Even better, some point to adult water baptism as proof of their salvation. But there are many who have a false, superstitious assurance of salvation resting in that action. Your Baptist friends would agree with you that their assurance, if not backed by a changed life, would be just as wrong as the superstitious beliefs of someone who relies on infant baptism for salvation.

"When you have an issue like this, Paul, it is very important to talk openly with people of different positions before you preach the sermon. Gather clues about their perceptions and arguments and attitudes. You cannot be too well prepared. And after all your work is done, remember to rest in the Lord. You don't need to force them into your belief. Let the Spirit of God work those changes."

The two were quiet now as the waitress brought the main courses. Paul had gone with a "safe" sweet-and-sour pork dinner while Dr. Vickerson tried out a new hot-and-spicy beef entrée. "The hotter the better!" he had aphoristically instructed the waitress.

After they had made considerable progress in their meal, Dr. Vickerson turned briefly to the matter of procedural sermons.

"The procedural sermon is a very practical 'how-to' message, Paul. It is usually topical in nature as it uses various portions of Scripture to gain a multifaceted insight into such issues as 'how to be a better parent,' 'how to study the Bible,' 'how to win over anger,' or 'how to forgive when you have been deeply wronged.'

"Procedural sermons are very popular because they speak directly to the believer's struggles, but they run the risk of being trite or contrived. To be done well, you need to spend much time in study and prayer. Try to dig deep, below the surface level.

"This is one of the few times when a preacher may need to number the points of the message. You know the danger of telling how many points the sermon has, Paul?"

"I've seen my congregation reach for their hymnbooks to find the last hymn as soon as I announce my final point."

"Right. When the preacher announces 'Finally...' or 'My last point today is...' the audience gets itself prepared to leave. Also, nothing seems more frustrating to the congregation than to hear the preacher go on for several more minutes after announcing the end of the message. So never, never number your points for the congregation unless you're giving them a step-by-step procedure, such as the reconciliation and discipline that Jesus outlines in Matthew 18 for us to follow."

The waitress interrupted again with two fortune cookies and the bill, which Dr. Vickerson quickly took from her. Paul was amazed at how fast his professor could move those frail, arthritic hands and joints when it came time to take the bill.

Dr. Vickerson lit up as he broke his fortune cookie in half in order to read the contents inside. "I remember eating Chinese food with my parents years ago. To me this was the best part of the meal! What does your fortune read, Paul?"

"It says, 'Walk a mile in my shoes before you criticize my position.'"

"It must have been written by a famous Chinese Indian!" Dr. Vickerson laughed. "But there is an important point there, Paul. That is excellent advice when you are preaching to persuade your congregation on some controversial topic. Put yourself thoroughly in the opposition's shoes before you preach the message. You must correctly understand the feelings and reasoning of the opposing viewpoint before you have the right to present your own."

"What does your fortune read, Dr. Vickerson?"

"Here, you'll have to read it for me; the print is too small."

Dr. Vickerson handed the tiny paper across the table and Paul read aloud, "The eagle never lost so much time as when he submitted to learn of the crow."

Dr. Vickerson's laughter puzzled Paul. He read the saying again to himself, while the professor rose slowly from the table.

"Don't you get it, Paul? You shouldn't be wasting your time learning from me! Your preaching is going to soar with the eagles, but this old crow is holding you back!"

"I hardly think of you as an old crow, sir," Paul responded. He smiled as he shook his head.

"Seriously, though, Paul, that's not a bad thought. You need to spend time studying the masters of preaching. Learn to soar with the eagles of the pulpit. When you get over to the library today check out a book or two of sermons. Use them in your devotional time, but also keep a critical eye open as to what techniques men like Calvin, Luther, Latimer, and Edwards used to communicate so effectively. Learn to soar with those eagles!"

After Dr. Vickerson paid the bill the two slowly made their way out to Paul's car.

As Paul dropped him off at the apartment, he remembered to give Dr. Vickerson the findings of his two-week time study. Then he headed for the seminary library to get his early start on Sunday's sermon and to pick up a few books of sermons to study.

13

Surprise Power

Paul's sermon series on Jonah was shaping up well. Because he had already done his exegesis of the first chapter, he could concentrate more on the creative arrangement of the data before him. It made him realize that starting on Monday for Sunday's sermon really wasn't early enough.

Then it hit him like a lightning bolt: "If I could only get two weeks ahead on exegesis! Imagine what I could do with all that extra time to prepare!"

After thinking about that for a moment he turned his attention to Jonah 1:6-12. Almost instantly an idea for Sunday's sermon flashed through his mind as he noticed four different questions asked of Jonah by the captain and his crew.

"Questions the world asks of the church," Paul muttered to himself.

"By grouping three of the questions in verse 8 as one I count six different questions. No, I'd better not number them, so the congregation doesn't anticipate the ending of my sermon," he said to himself as he remembered the conversation over lunch.

The six questions that Paul used that Sunday were these:

1. How is it that you are sleeping? (verse 6).
2. On whose account has this tragedy struck us? (verse 8).
3. What is your occupation? (verse 8).
4. Where do you come from? What is your country? From what people are you? (verse 8).
5. How could you do this? (verse 10).
6. What should we do to you that the sea may become calm for us? (verse 11).

With these questions before him Paul began to see all kinds of possibilities for his message. His biggest problem would be to limit himself. Perhaps Dr. Vickerson might see a series of six sermons instead of just one!

He was amazed at how different these questions were compared to the ordinary thinking in the church. The storm at sea was more an act of judgment on Jonah than on the ungodly sailors. The question is not "What will God do to sinners?" but "What should we sinners do to this saint to calm the sea?" Paul wondered aloud how much the storms of life in our society are more to be blamed on the failure and disobedience of God's people than on the sinful world. The whole message had an ironic twist. Everything was turned upside-down.

When Paul came to Dr. Vickerson's apartment the following Monday he could hardly contain his excitement as he placed his sermon notes before his professor.

The elderly man shared his excitement. It was so good to see Paul's joy of preaching restored. Here was a man who had lost confidence in his preaching abilities, had lost the zeal of his early years fresh out of seminary, and had become stale and dull in the pulpit; yet almost overnight a transformation was taking place.

"Dr. Vickerson, I know the Lord inspired me to prepare this message. It seemed to jump right out at me."

"I agree with you, Paul. Usually agony and hard work are required, but sometimes inspiration comes in a flurry like that. The Lord gave you an extra boost this week."

"The congregation liked it a lot. I received more compliments than in years," Paul bubbled on. "There were some out-of-town visitors on Sunday, and one lady was certain it was a pulpit committee. She said, 'I hope you don't have plans of leaving us, Pastor. Your preaching is so powerful.'"

"That's so good to hear," Dr. Vickerson responded. "I have been praying daily for your work, Paul."

Dr. Vickerson's disclosure surprised Paul; he never thought of his professor praying for him. The revelation momentarily overwhelmed him. He tried to casually wipe the corner of his eyes with the back of his hand.

"You have discovered several principles that unleash power and bring freshness to your preaching," Dr. Vickerson continued, sensing that it was time to press on.

"I have?" Paul asked. "What exactly have I discovered?"

"First of all, you have employed what Charles Spurgeon called 'surprise power.'"

Paul wrote "surprise power" in his notebook.

"Surprise power," Dr. Vickerson continued, "is that element of Scripture that leaps out and startles the attentive reader. The problem is that we often don't allow the full impact of a passage to grip us. Perhaps we're dull of hearing, or perhaps we have heard it read so often that we don't allow it to sink into our minds."

"Can you give me some examples of surprise power?" Paul asked.

"You used it on Sunday. You saw how ironic, how strangely different, the questions were. It was the world grieving and horrified at the sins of God's people rather than God's people grieving over the sins of the world. It was the world suffering God's judgment because of the sins of the believer rather than the believer suffering from the sins of the world. That is a strange twist. That's surprise power."

"It surprised me to see it. I have read Jonah at least two dozen times in my life, but I never saw it before."

Surprise power is that element of Scripture that leaps out and startles the attentive reader.

"That's what I mean about surprise power; sometimes we're so dulled to it. Let me give you an example of a surprise power sermon I once gave. It was on Titus 1. Do you remember that amazing quote Paul cites about the people of Crete?"

"Yes, and I was always a little troubled by it," Paul answered. "He said, 'Cretans are always liars, evil beasts, and lazy gluttons.'"

"Very good. It is surprising and disturbing. I haven't heard many sermons on it, have you, Paul? Yet we often miss gold mines by avoiding difficult passages. Serious Christians want these texts explained. You will have a ready audience when your sermon wrestles with those difficulties."

"But it has to be done well," Paul responded. "I failed miserably in my attempts to explain millennial views."

"Yes, your explanations can be far too technical and detailed. And the congregation has to see some application or usefulness in the matter, or else it appears to be the idle speculations of theologians."

"Angels dancing on pinheads," Paul added.

"We're digressing a little," Dr. Vickerson said, glancing at his watch. "Back to Titus. The real surprise power in Titus is not so much that difficult quote about the Cretans. The real surprise power comes when you compare that quote with what preceded it. Do you remember the opening verses of Titus 1?"

"They deal with qualifications for elders. I pass those verses out every year to our new church officers."

"Very good. I had also read that passage dozens of times, just like you read Jonah, before it finally leaped out at me one day. How could Titus find any godly men in Crete? Who could be qualified to serve if 'Cretans are always liars, evil beasts, lazy gluttons?' How can Titus find godly leadership in a place like Crete?"

"Hmmmm! I never thought of that before," said Paul.

"I never connected the two either. But as soon as I did, all kinds of lights flashed on inside me. For example, what kind of person was Titus? Paul entrusted him with such a difficult place as Crete. Search out Titus in the rest of the New Testament, and you will be amazed at how he was used by the apostle to carry out his ministry."

"I don't remember much about Titus," Paul admitted.

"You'll have to do a little study. The real surprise power in this passage is found in the gospel itself. Titus 1:2 speaks of the hope of eternal life promised by a God who, unlike the lying Cretans, cannot lie. I used this message at the ordination of one of my former seminary students. Do you know Dan Clarke?"

"No, I don't think so," Paul answered.

"No? He must have graduated before you did. Well, I asked Dan if he really believed in the power of the gospel— power to change liars, gluttons, and evil beasts into men, women, and children of God. I challenged him to set up church in the midst of hell. I reminded him that Jesus promised that the gates of hell could not prevail against the church of Jesus Christ!"

"That *is* powerful, Dr. Vickerson!" said Paul as he wrote some notes on a future sermon idea.

"That's surprise power at work," Dr. Vickerson emphasized. "The Bible is full of it, if you open your eyes to see it. There is the Prodigal Son's father racing out to meet him. He is not supposed to do that. There is a Samaritan who turns out to be the hero. That's not the way it is supposed to be. There is the shock of being told that our righteousness must surpass that of the scribes and Pharisees. The people must have reeled from that remark, for who then could be saved?"

Dr. Vickerson continued with more examples. "There are little surprises found tucked away all through Scriptures. Who was that young man who fled right out of his robe into the night at the arrest of Jesus? Was it Mark? What about those 'other little boats' that accompanied the disciples' boat when Jesus was awakened to calm the storm? Why are they mentioned? Even the genealogy of Jesus contains its surprises with skeletons in the closet like Rahab the harlot, Tamar, and Bathsheba."

"How did Dan Clarke respond to that ordination message from Titus, Dr. Vickerson?"

"Funny you should ask. Dan started out as an assistant pastor in charge of youth ministry in a rather wealthy suburban church. But a few years later he accepted a challenge from his denomination to become a church planter in a tough inner-city area noted for its crime and drug problems. At the time of their move, I received a brief note from Dan's wife, Charlene. All it said was, 'Dan wanted you to have our new address and to inform you that he is setting up church in the middle of hell!' "

"Wow! It must make you feel good to know you had that kind of effect upon his ministry."

"Oh, I imagine if the Lord wanted Dan Clarke in the inner city He would have managed to get him there quite easily without my influence. But, yes, I do feel good about it."

"How is his work going? Have you heard from him lately?"

"No. I'm afraid our move to Phoenix succeeded in severing a lot of communication lines, including that of the Clarkes. The last I heard they were off to a slow but solid start and had been used by the Lord in a few dramatic conversions.

"Maybe someday I'll take the time to find out how they're doing; but now back to you, Paul. Search for the surprise power in God's Word. Our God is a surprising God. His Word and His world are full of marvelous surprises. All too often the preacher of the Word strains out the delicious wonders and serves it up with boring dullness, drained of all life! The Word of God must surprise *you* first, so it can surprise God's people who hear you."

14

Creating Internal Dialogue

"In addition to 'surprise power' your sermon also shows you the power of questions, Paul. By asking those questions found in Jonah 1:6-12 you stimulate your people to answer in their minds. This is a great method for holding their attention. Have you ever noticed how often Jesus used questions when talking to His audience?"

"Quite honestly, I never thought much about it before."

"I have the number right here in my notebook," Dr. Vickerson said as he tapped his index finger on the yellowing pages of his notes. "Do you realize that in the Gospel accounts there are 237 questions recorded on the lips of our Lord? And hardly one of them is asked in order to gather information.

"There is great searching and convicting power in a question. For example, Jesus spoke of loving our enemies in Matthew 5. He first illustrated how the Father does so by sending the rain on just and unjust alike; then He drove home the point with a series of poignant questions.

"Listen to His words in verses 46 and 47, Paul:

> If you love those who love you, what reward have you? Do not even the tax-gatherers do the same? And if you greet your brothers only, what do you do more than others? Do not even the Gentiles do the same?

"Sense how the knife cuts deeper to the heart with a question instead of an assertive statement. Can you feel its blade plunging deeper with each additional question?"

"I see what you mean," Paul replied. "Instead of just telling the people how they should think, Jesus asked them to search their own souls to see if they were in right relation to God."

"Yes. It would be a good exercise for you to reread the Gospels and mark each one of Jesus' questions. Ask yourself what the effect of the question was, and how a straightforward assertive statement might have weakened the point. Someday you might even preach a series on 'Questions Jesus Asks of You.'"

"With 237 of them, I could preach for quite some time!" Paul laughed.

"Jesus also ended some of His parables with a question," Dr. Vickerson hurried on. "In the Good Samaritan parable He did not merely assert 'You ought to go help your neighbor.' He asked instead, 'Which of these three do you think proved to be a neighbor to the man who fell into the robbers' hands?' The question forced the Jews to acknowledge the Samaritan."

"What about the prophets, Dr. Vickerson? Prophetic preaching has a searching characteristic to it, so questions would seem to be appropriate."

"An excellent observation, Paul. You're quite right. In fact, the book you're preaching on now even *ends* with a question. Read it for yourself."

Paul turned to Jonah 4:11 and read:

> Should I not have compassion on Nineveh, the great city in which there are more than 120,000 persons who do not know the difference between their right and left hand, as well as many animals?

"What a powerful ending to this excellent book!" Dr. Vickerson exclaimed. "Jonah is left to sit beside his wilted gourd, in the middle of the hot desert, and ponder the love of God for the lost people of the world."

"In that case the prophet is being searched by the question rather than doing the searching," Paul observed.

"That's true, but if you look at the ending of Nahum it's the opposite, yet concerning the same city, Nineveh. Listen to the haunting nature of Nahum's query:

> There is no relief for your breakdown, your wound is incurable. All who hear about you will clap their hands over you, for on whom has not your evil passed continually?

"Again, it's a perfect ending to a book predicting judgment about to fall on a city.

"Paul, you're learning fast about the power of questions. An important effect of using questions in your sermons is that it causes the people to carry on a dialogue with you as you preach. Occasionally someone might even respond aloud, but usually the conversation takes place inside their heads."

"Now that you mention it, I've heard some ministers encourage their people to answer aloud from time to time. They repeat their questions until the people give a strong response."

"Yes, and they do it to keep their people with them and to emphasize an important point. Watch your people when you ask questions. Some will nod their heads, while others may look puzzled as they think about an answer. You can tell immediately if they're with you, if they're listening, and if they understand.

"Some questions may only be along the lines of 'Do you understand what I'm saying?' They help you check on your audience at a point of difficulty. Other questions may suggest, 'Did you hear what I said?' They help you accent an important truth that you don't want people to miss."

"That's kind of the way Jesus used 'truly, truly' or 'let him who has ears to hear,'" Paul responded as he hastily wrote notes to himself about the purpose of questions.

"Right, although those aren't actually questions, they act mostly as attention arresters. Another reason to use a question might be to ask the obvious rather than to state it—more of a rhetorical question.

"But remember the effect of questions: They ask your audience to *think and answer*, not just listen. They stimulate their minds to answer back inside their heads. As long as the people are in dialogue with you in their thoughts, you have them listening. They are paying attention and their minds are less prone to wandering.

Instead of just telling the people how they should think, Jesus asked them to search their own souls to see if they were in right relation to God.

"The same is true when you use puzzles, riddles, and brainteasers. If you ask someone a puzzling question or present a riddle to him, he instinctively rises to the challenge in an attempt to solve the problem. Again, he is interacting with you, if only in his head."

"The only riddle that comes immediately to mind is Samson's puzzle about the lion and the honey. Are there others in the Bible?" Paul asked.

"In a way all of Jesus' parables were puzzles or riddles. Remember how the disciples frequently came to Him later for an explanation of what He meant? Think of how long their curiosity was at work trying to solve the mystery before He revealed its solution."

"So riddles and puzzles had a more lasting effect than straight questions, since the crowds went away thinking for days about what a certain parable actually meant."

"Right. Also, think of how that technique would fix the parable and its interpretation in the disciples' minds once Jesus revealed its solution. If you have ever worked hard at unraveling a brainteaser or a puzzle, you know how all that effort has a way of engraving the solution forever in your mind. The next time someone tries to trick you with it, you usually remember the solution immediately."

Paul thought of how many hours it took him to solve Rubic's cube and how he hadn't picked one up in over two years. He wondered how long it would take for the solution to come back to him.

"One of my favorite examples of the Lord's riddles is found in Mark 12:35-37," Dr. Vickerson said as he turned to it in his timeworn Bible.

Paul thought of how the old Bible was about as fragile as the professor himself. He wondered to himself if Dr. Vickerson's voice didn't seem weaker to him today than last week.

"Look at this masterful passage from the Master Himself," Dr. Vickerson continued, unaware of Paul's thoughts

How is it that the scribes say that the Christ
is the son of David? David himself said in the

Holy Spirit, "The Lord said to my Lord, 'Sit at My right hand until I put Thine enemies beneath Thy feet.'" David himself calls him "Lord"; and so in what sense is He his son?

"Mark follows this with the observation that the common people heard him gladly. But can you imagine what this did to the religious leaders? It put them right in the middle of a puzzle, the obvious solution of which was the Messianic nature of Jesus Christ. It was a puzzle they didn't want to solve; in fact Matthew tells us they dared not ask Jesus any more questions and refused to answer Him a word."

Dr. Vickerson leafed through his notebook. "Here it is," he said, as if Paul knew what he was looking for. "Jeremias gives several other examples of the use of riddles by Jesus. How could John the baptist be the greatest of men born to women, but the least in the kingdom of God? What about Jesus' cryptic remarks about 'Destroy this temple, and in three days I will rebuild it?' He also cites the three kinds of eunuchs in Matthew 19:12 as another riddle."

"What about posing our own riddles to the congregation?" Paul asked.

"Sometimes you can draw them from Scripture itself. For example, when God speaks of 'us' in Genesis 1:26 and 11:7, who is He talking to? If you ask that of your people, they begin to see the doctrine of the trinity veiled in Old Testament language."

"How about contrasting Ephesians 2:8,9 with James' words about a man being justified 'by works and not by faith alone'?" Paul suggested.

"Excellent. One of the most gripping messages you can preach is when you can hold up two apparently contradictory passages or truths of Scripture, let the congregation struggle with the tension for awhile, then help them solve the problem. Some churchgoers have sat in the pews for years waiting for an explanation of how you can never be separated from the love of God, when the writer of Hebrews warns against apostasy and falling away. They are waiting, but most preachers fear to venture into these areas."

"Maybe they themselves don't know the answer. You can't expect a preacher to preach what he doesn't know!" Paul exclaimed.

"No, don't ever preach if you're uncertain about the major truth of your message. Sadly, though, most preachers don't preach on these problems because their schedules are too filled with busywork instead of the Lord's work. It takes time, hard labor, and agony to search out answers to some of these matters. But instead of spending time feeding deeply on the Word of God, many preachers are still feeding off their seminary training many years after seminary. No wonder their messages are stale and powerless!"

"Speaking of schedules, can we talk about that time study before I head for the library?" Paul asked. Dr. Vickerson's remarks about time and misplaced priorities triggered Paul's memory about the assignment he had turned in the week before.

"By all means. We need to get you prepared to face your Board. When is your next meeting?"

"Not until late August, when we meet to discuss plans for the fall season."

"Those plans need to include some changes in your own schedule. Now would be a good time to get started on it."

Dr. Vickerson rose slowly to get Paul's time study from his office desk. As he reached for his cane the phone in the kitchen began to ring. Both he and Paul jumped, startled by its sudden interruption.

"Now who would be calling me? I get so few phone calls anymore."

Sensing the time and effort it would take Dr. Vickerson to reach the phone, Paul rose and answered for him. The caller was Arlene, Paul's secretary. She hated to bother him, but there was an emergency—a genuine one. Mildred Lyons had just called the church office to say that Larry had suffered a heart attack while out on the golf course. He was in critical condition in the intensive-care ward of the hospital, and Mildred wanted Paul to come immediately.

"Larry was chairman of the pulpit committee. He stopped attending church weeks ago because of all the criticism surrounding my poor preaching," Paul explained.

"That's sad about his heart attack. I'll keep him in my prayers," Dr. Vickerson said, shaking his head.

Paul quickly gathered his Bible and notebook and headed for the hospital.

15

The Nehemiah Project

As Paul sped toward the hospital his instincts told him that this was going to be one of those weeks in a pastor's life. It would be easy to allow the events before him to crowd out time for serious sermon preparation, so he made a promise to himself that he would get up earlier each day if necessary to find time for it.

Not only did Larry Lyons undergo emergency triple bypass surgery, but Paul had the funeral of an elderly shut-in as well as a wedding. Both fell on Saturday.

The whole week was a flurry of activity. Plans had to be made for a funeral meal at the church on Saturday, then a quick shuffling of the fellowship hall for a wedding reception that evening. On Friday night he managed to squeeze in a stop at the funeral home between the rehearsal and the rehearsal dinner. Meanwhile he traveled back and forth daily to check Larry's progress and to comfort Mildred during the ordeal.

Paul had mixed emotions while visiting the Lyons family. Here was the man who had been so excited to extend the call to the Andrews to come to Calvary Church. Paul remembered the rainy night that Larry and Mildred had showed up with a whole crew of members from the church to help move him from the seminary apartment to their home near the church.

Then he thought of Larry dropping out of the church over embarrassment at Paul's lackluster performance in the pulpit. Secretly, he wondered what Larry might do if he survived his heart surgery. Would he feel so indebted that he would return to church? Or would he continue to stay away?

In between times, he kept his promise to work on Sunday's sermon, rising two hours earlier on Tuesday, Wednesday, and Thursday to devote precious energies to his preparation.

Two months earlier, Paul would have let the whole thing slide into Saturday night after the reception, then excuse himself for a dismal Sunday message on the basis of the added activities of the week. After all, his people often encouraged that attitude by sympathizing with him at the door after such a hectic week.

But he was now recommitted to the importance of preaching. He would rise earlier, if necessary, to find time to prepare.

"I can't believe how motivated I was last week," Paul said to the old professor. Dr. Vickerson expressed delight over Paul's rekindled enthusiasm. "I didn't allow my preaching to suffer drastically despite all the emergencies. I was even able to blend some of the events of the week into the sermon in a way that brought a deeper significance to both the message and the life of our congregation."

"Don't neglect your rest, Paul," Dr. Vickerson warned. "We can ride the crest of emotions for only so long.

Remember how Jesus had His disciples come apart with Him to a lonely place, before they came apart at the seams? Take this week to breathe.

"Just as your sermon preparation must follow that attack-rest-attack-rest pattern, your body needs it too. Spend extra time with your family. Take an extra day or at least a half-day off. Better to come back anxious to get on with your work than to wear out and begin to dread the hours."

"I know from experience that you're right, Dr. Vickerson. Thanks for reminding me. It helps me not to feel so guilty if I do rest a little."

"Good. Now on with the work of preaching. You'll need to wait until tomorrow for that rest," Dr. Vickerson laughed.

"We were just beginning to talk about the Board meeting when the phone interrupted us last week. I've been so curious to hear your ideas."

"All right, let's begin. Your time study revealed the normal kinds of problems that pastors face. In your head you know that your training and heart's desire has been to minister the Word, to preach and to pray, as Acts 6 puts it. But the reality of the pastorate puts you under constant strain. There is that tug-of-war going on between 'real' ministry and 'church work.' Unless you define your calling clearly, outlining your areas of responsibility, then scheduling your priorities accordingly, you'll never get around to those high-priority areas."

"Who was it that talked about the tyranny of the urgent?" Paul asked. "The urgent is seldom important, the important is seldom urgent."

"I think it was Paul Little, and I agree with him. Jesus made a conscientious effort to avoid the time trap. He was too active in His Father's business to become sidetracked. Isn't it amazing that when He came to the end of His public ministry He acknowledged before His Father that He had done everything the Father had sent Him to do?"

"I feel like I seldom get done what the Father wants *me* to do!"

"You never will until you stop listening to the countless bosses you have and listen to your Master's voice. You cannot serve two masters."

"How will I ever learn to do that?" Paul asked.

"Part of the problem is your insecurity toward other people. Ministers especially find it hard to say no to the many requests that come their way. We long to be nice guys, loved by all. But If you know your calling, and have a sure understanding of who you are in Christ, you can stand more firmly in it. You can learn to politely refuse to do the business that others in the church should rightly do."

Jesus made a conscientious effort to avoid the time trap. He was too active in His Father's business to become sidetracked.

"For example?" Paul asked.

"For example, writing and editing the newsletter. Is there no one else in the church who could do that job? Did you see how many hours you gave to the newsletter the two weeks you kept your log? And that's a monthly obligation, isn't it?"

"Yes, except for August. But I don't mind doing the newsletter."

"It's not a matter of *minding*; it is a matter of *priorities*." Dr. Vickerson remarked.

"But I don't think anyone else would really—"

"—do as well as you?" The professor completed Paul's thoughts.

"Well, that's part of it. I'm afraid it might not get done at all. The church had no newsletter for a couple of years, so finally I took it on. I felt it was important."

"The same for the lawn-mowing?" Dr. Vickerson pressed on.

"I couldn't stand the witness to the neighbors. The grass had been neglected for two weeks, and we had all that rain. Besides, it was good exercise for me," Paul protested.

"Let the grass grow!" Dr. Vickerson roared. The force of his voice took Paul back. "Paul, you are neglecting the Word of God to serve tables!"

"Doesn't cutting the grass set myself as an example of servanthood? I think it encourages others to follow my lead." Paul was feeling a little hurt. Dr. Vickerson seemed a little less patient than usual this morning.

"Has anyone else come up to you to take over the job?"

"No, not yet."

"And I bet you like to shovel snow in the winter months, too."

"How'd you guess that? Yes, I do. And while we're on the subject, I spent the first week of July repainting my office. I enjoy that kind of work. At least I can see immediate, visible results if I paint or cut the grass. I often work with people for years and see nothing!"

"But no one else has followed your example and come to your aid? Don't you see, Paul? The more work like that you do, the more they expect it of you. Besides, I'll bet there are a number of projects around your own home that Susan has been after you to complete. Right?"

"She was a little upset about my painting the office, since she's been after me to paint her laundry room for several weeks now."

"She has a right to be upset, Paul. Listen, you were gifted by God to be a servant of the Word of God. That is your servanthood. That is why you rose early last week to make sure your message was ready for Sunday. Don't you ever feel resentful about doing those other things—Painting, mowing, shoveling snow, writing the newsletter, and taking out the garbage for the church?"

"Occasionally I get resentful, but I attribute that to my own sinful nature," Paul confessed.

"Your resentment may also be an instinctive reaction to the fact that you are out of your calling, while others are neglecting theirs. It might even stem from the convicting of the Holy Spirit. There are dozens of people in your church capable of cutting grass and shoveling snow. If they won't do it, then put it in the budget and pay someone else to do it. But don't neglect your calling to serve tables."

"I know you're right, but sometimes I can't stand to see the neglect of the building and grounds."

"Let it go, but communicate at the same time why you're letting it go. Your people are smart enough to understand, but you have to communicate the issue effectively to them.

"Another time-waster I noticed was one you pointed to a while back," Dr. Vickerson continued. "You allow office drop-ins who seem to have nothing better to do than sit around and shoot the breeze. You need to find ways to limit that."

"But our people insist on having a minister who is accessible, easy to talk to, available for counsel." Paul agreed with Dr. Vickerson on this issue, but he couldn't see any clear solution.

"Again, it's important to communicate, and to communicate carefully. You don't want to give the impression that you're too busy for genuine needs, but you do want people to know the value of your time. It's one thing to counsel, another to waste time.

"But there's a deeper problem underneath all this, Paul. As it stands now you have little respect from your people. They may pay lip service, but they really value neither your time nor your high calling. You are the man who doesn't have anything to do after Sundays are over. You must change that image! Not defensively or impatiently, but you must change it."

"What's the plan?" Paul asked. "What do you suggest?"

"First, become convinced in your own mind. You may be able to write a better newsletter than anyone else in the church. You may be able to paint and shovel snow and cut grass very well, but those are not your responsibilities. You may be great at killing time in pleasant conversation, but your time is too valuable to kill. You are to *redeem* the time, not waste it.

"So get your priorities straight in your own mind. Use that list which separates the things *you* should do from the things *others* should do. Remember Acts 6 and Ephesians 4. You owe God first. You owe God your best with the gifts of your calling.

"Then go before the Board with all your ducks in line. But before you do that, it would be good to take some additional preparatory steps. Are there some members of your Board you can deeply trust and to whom you can share your heart?" Dr. Vickerson asked.

"In these kinds of matters I can think of three or four," Paul answered.

"Good. Sit down with them separately or even together over breakfast or lunch someday. Show them the materials you've gathered. Give them your observations on what you've discovered concerning the use of your time.

"Then ask them—and I think this is important, Paul—ask them, 'How do you view my calling as your pastor?' Ask them why they think you went to seminary. Ask them what they think your special training involved. What was the purpose of learning Greek and Hebrew, homiletics, church history, theology, and ethics?

"You don't want to convey an air of superiority, but you do need to communicate the deep conviction of your calling and training. You want to do what you were called and trained to do."

Paul could see the point of asking it that way. The questions had obvious answers to them. Why should he have taken all that specialized training if he doesn't have time to use it? What good are God's gifts to the church if he never has time to use them?

"After you get those few to see the problem, then plan with them to go before the whole Board with the same materials."

"Dr. Vickerson, do you think it would be wise for them to prepare the Board a little ahead of time, so they aren't taken back by any surprises?"

"That would help as long as your confidants are good communicators. They should not put others on the defensive, but sincerely share your concern. Yes, that would be excellent."

"What should I expect them to do with it?" Paul asked.

"They can act in several ways. First, they can clarify your present job description or work together with you to write a new one. Second, they can commit themselves to filling in the voids that your changes will create. They can communicate those needs to the congregation and encourage others to come forward to help.

"And Paul, don't make the mistake of thinking an announcement in the bulletin or a column in the newsletter is enough. It is almost impossible to overcommunicate in the church."

"What else can be done?" Paul asked.

"One of the best things your Board can do for you is run your interference. It is a lot better for a time-waster to be given some kind hints from a Board member than from you. They should take time in their conversations to build up your unique role in the church while alerting others not to infringe upon that role. Let them run interference for you.

"Don't omit your secretary, either. Arlene can do you a great deal of good by screening phone calls and office visits. I know of one pastor who devotes his mornings to study. The congregation knows not to interrupt him except for bona fide emergencies. His secretary relays his messages to him at 11:00 A.M. and even dials the numbers for him in order to save his time if the line is busy or if the other party is not able to answer the call back.

"And if someone needs an appointment, he has given her enough time slots to fill so that she can do that for him. Then she alerts him to the appointments she has scheduled."

"That sounds like a big help. My main need is to explain all this to the Board and my secretary and the church so they understand what I'm trying to do, and why I'm trying to do it," Paul commented.

"Communication is vital, but don't you think it will make sense to them, Paul? Just having them think about why you received all that training should get them started in the right direction."

"I know of one colleague of mine who schedules his appointments backward," Paul remembered. "He has the secretary book the first appointment at 4:00 or 4:30 P.M., the second just before it, and so forth back to 1:00 P.M. He says this gives him extra time to study and write in the afternoon. What do you think of that idea, Dr. Vickerson?"

"I think it depends somewhat on the individual pastor. I found that my mind was fairly full and tired by lunchtime, so I tried to schedule appointments over lunch and during the afternoon. I could come back to my studies later, having given my mind a few hours' rest. But experiment to see what works best for you."

"So that's my basic strategy for the Board meeting?" Paul asked.

"Yes, you can fill in the details. But by all means don't surprise them with this on the night of the meeting. First work with those few that you think would be most sympathetic to your ideas. Then alert the others ahead of time so that it will be on the agenda. After that you can go to the meeting prepared to make some major changes in your pastoral role. Go in faith, attended by prayer. But be sure you've done all your homework."

Dr. Vickerson paused, then added, "Do it the way Nehemiah did."

"How's that?" Paul asked.

"Remember how he arose in the night and went out with a few trusted men to inspect the wall of Jerusalem? He surveyed the problem, gathered the data, formulated his plans, shared them only with those trusted men, then went to the people with his plan of action. He was very wise. It would do you well to follow his example. You could call this your Nehemiah Project."

16

Surprising Requests

"I think we've said enough for now about the Church Board, don't you?" Dr. Vickerson took off his wire-rims and rubbed his tired eyes. He grew uncharacteristically solemn.

"I agree. I almost feel like I've just gone through another Board meeting," Paul laughed, unaware yet of his mentor's mood.

The old man sat in silence for a moment, then put his glasses back on.

"I have a favor to ask of you, Paul. This might seem strange, but I want you to preach at my funeral."

Instinctively Paul started to protest, but Dr. Vickerson waved him off.

"Hear me out first. I'm very serious about this. Years ago a colleague of mine made an agreement with me. Joe and I met in seminary and have stayed close through the years. We agreed that whoever outlived the other would conduct the other's funeral. At first it was more of a joke than an agreement. But the more we joked about it the more we knew we both really meant it. Shortly after you left my apartment last week I received a phone call that he had died suddenly in his sleep. I preached at his funeral on Thursday."

"I'm sorry, Dr. Vickerson. I was so caught up in sharing my own activities of the past week that I didn't realize until now what you've been going through."

"I intended to tell you first thing this morning, but you arrived here in such an excited state that I couldn't spoil your joy. I do mean business about having you preach at my funeral, though," Dr. Vickerson said firmly. "I can think of no other living soul I would rather have do it than you."

Paul struggled to find an appropriate response. "I'm honored by your request. I don't know what more to say."

"Say nothing more!" the old man brightened a little. "I have written down my desires for the memorial service. Please put this in a safe place until you have need of it."

He handed Paul a business-size envelope with the words "The Memorial Service of Dr. William Vickerson" handwritten neatly across the front of it. Paul lingered over the envelope much longer than it took to read its title, then carefully secured it between the pages of his Bible.

"I also have a second request to ask of you," Dr. Vickerson continued. "Last evening an idea came to me concerning our work here together. I was reading in 2 Timothy 2. It was the second verse that set my mind to thinking about this matter."

The two men turned to the passage and Dr. Vickerson read from his old Bible:

> The things which you have heard from me in the presence of many witnesses, these entrust to faithful men, who will be able to teach others also.

He repeated it again, then slowly closed his Bible.

As Paul studied the face across from him he wondered how he was so insensitive not to see sooner the obvious sorrow it bore. Then Dr. Vickerson's voice drew him back to the issue at hand.

"It occurred to me last night that you are like Timothy to me. You have become my dear son during our time together. Paul, I want you to do for me what the apostle instructed Timothy to do for him. I want you to share your experience here with other pastors who need encouragement and help in their preaching."

"You mean invite others to join here with me on Monday mornings?"

"No, I was thinking that you could develop a small course or a seminar on preaching—one you would teach to your peers. You could create it out of the materials from your notes with a focus on ways to recapture freshness and zeal in preaching."

Paul reacted strongly. "Who am I to suddenly become an expert on preaching? It's one thing to take notes for myself, but to teach others—that's different!"

"Think about it, Paul. It has been so rewarding for me to see the change in you, and I don't have time or energy left to do this for many others. I thought maybe you could do it for me. After all, isn't this what the apostle was experiencing when he wrote 2 Timothy? He was at the end of his course and concerned that the work would continue after his departure. So he entrusted Timothy with the task of teaching others, who in turn were to train still others."

"Let me look back over my notes and see what I can do," Paul responded weakly. "I'll think about it."

"I'll work with you on it, son. You admit there's a great need for this, don't you?"

"Yes, I agree. I know several pastors who could use the same boost to their preaching that you've given mine."

"Then it's settled! You can begin with those you know."

"But I'm not the right person for the job. *You're* the professor of homiletics, not me."

"You don't have to pose as a great authority on preaching; just share your own story. Your rekindled enthusiasm will be credentials enough. Teach others what you've been learning here, and encourage *them* to teach others in turn. Inspiring preaching is the need of the hour in the church, and by God's grace you can help meet that need."

Suddenly Paul had an inspiration. The idea had been in the back of his mind for a few weeks, and perhaps this would give him a way out of this dilemma.

"Dr. Vickerson, what if I taught a class to my Sunday school teachers on the principles you've been sharing with me? What I mean is this: Awhile back my Sunday school superintendent told me he was having trouble filling the various classes with teacher positions. The teachers are tired and want a rest."

"Of course these principles would work well with teaching, too," Dr. Vickerson responded. "For years I was an annual speaker at the state Sunday School Convention, where I led various seminars on teaching God's Word with enthusiasm and creativity."

Paul brightened, "Did the people respond well to your seminars?"

"They asked me back every year until my retirement."

"I guess they benefited from it!" Paul laughed. "So you would allow a teacher training course to fulfill your request?"

As Paul looked thoughtfully into his professor's face, he could see that the offer was not enough to satisfy him. Dr. Vickerson's eyes silently pleaded for Paul's commitment.

After a long pause, Paul answered his own question. "I'll work on it, and I promise to give it my best."

"Thank you, son. Nothing could please me more at this point in my life."

Then with a slight smile Dr. Vickerson raised his hand and added, "And Paul, please do that teacher training class, too. Your people will be endeared to you for the help."

Inspiring preaching is the need of the hour in the church, and by God's grace you can help meet that need.

17

Reservoir Power

The events surrounding the funeral of Dr. Vickerson's friend tired and drained him. Paul offered to leave so he could get some rest, but he insisted on discussing one other critical matter.

"I must talk to you about 'Reservoir Power,' since I believe it to be the most important ingredient in preaching. Reservoir Power will not only give you a significant boost, but it will also help guard against the crude manipulation of certain principles of preaching, resulting in sermons devoid of the Spirit of God.

"Paul, what do you think of when you hear the term 'reservoir'?"

"I think of an artificial lake or a water dam."

"Very good. Bernard of Clairvaux once offered an excellent analogy contrasting reservoirs with water pipes."

Dr. Vickerson read from his notes:

> If then you are wise you will show yourself
> rather as a reservoir than as a water pipe. For a
> pipe spreads abroad water as it receives it, but
> a reservoir waits till it is filled to overflowing,
> and thus communicates without loss to itself
> its superabundance of water.

"Let me tell you what I think he means. The water pipe delivers as it draws from another source, a little at a time. If that other source is cut off, it soon runs dry. It has no reserve supply from which to draw.

"The reservoir also draws its water from another source, but with a significant difference: It gathers great quantities of water until it is filled to overflowing. From the overflow it supplies others. If its source is suddenly cut off, it can continue to supply water for long periods of time until fresh rains replenish it.

"Preachers ought to be more like great reservoirs than mere water pipes. They should operate out of the fullness of God's presence in their lives rather than operating on the margin."

"I think I know what you're saying, but could you please explain the concept a little more fully?" Paul asked. "After all, I would be better able to explain it to those in my seminar."

"If the supply you receive from God's Word is immediately passed on to the people in your ministry, then you will always be depleting yourself of the resources needed to carry on the work. This is the pattern of too many pastors. Their weekly studies meet only their weekly needs—the Sunday sermon or sermons, the weekly Bible study, perhaps a Sunday school class or a small group meeting. At the end of each week they have given out all that they had taken in. They are empty again and must begin the scramble to find fresh supplies for the coming week. What they should really be doing is filling up the reservoir and allowing its abundance to overflow to their people."

"I admit that this has been my own pattern of study," Paul confessed. "I usually expend all my efforts on the very lessons and sermons I deliver in any given week. So how do I change my habits from a water pipe ministry to a reservoir ministry? How do I go about filling the reservoir?" He sketched a reservoir in his notes in anticipation of Dr. Vickerson's answer.

"First, don't fail to fill the reservoir with enough study and serious reflection on the weekly sermon itself. You should so overflow with an abundance of truth discovered in the sermon preparation that your people sense that when you've finished preaching you have not given them everything you could have. They should realize that if time permitted there would be even more wonderful streams of truth flowing from the pulpit.

"Much of the preaching I hear is so shallow, so superficial. It only skims the surface of the Scripture, never digging deep enough to expose its hidden treasures. The congregation know that a cursory reading of the passage on their own would produce almost as much insight as they heard from the pulpit. What they have experienced is more like a trickle than the overflowing from a reservoir's abundance."

"I know what you mean," Paul responded. "I have a Sunday school teacher who never prepares his lesson. He uses the excuse that he is relying on the Holy Spirit to lead the study."

"And how well is his class attended?"

"Only a handful come, more out of duty than desire."

"Just as I expected. Did you ever notice how often the Holy Spirit fails to lead such efforts? Why should God bless laziness?

"On the other hand, Paul, I know you have also experienced the exhilaration that comes from discovering the deep, hidden treasures of God's Word, treasures that cannot be unearthed by a half-hearted effort using a child's toy shovel. And when you preached, your excitement over those discoveries could not help but bubble up and spill forth from the pulpit to your people."

Paul nodded in agreement while Dr. Vickerson continued.

"So don't neglect serious and scholarly study. Extra work helps to fill up the reservoir while adding a significant dimension to your preaching. People know the difference between half-hearted preparation and an all-out effort to find God's truth."

"I know what you mean, but sometimes the things that inspire *me* leave my people flat. What's the difference between scholarship that excites people and scholarship that bores them?"

"An excellent question, Paul. I can answer much of it in one word: trivia! The devil delights in getting us to play Trivial Pursuit in a sermon, and encourages us to parade that knowledge before the people for the sake of elevating self rather than God. Of course it is just as easy to pride ourselves in communicating pertinent and practical knowledge, but that kind of knowledge carries a force with it that directs the hearers away from the preacher and more to the Lord. God can be glorified in that practical kind of truth even though the preacher might be seeking to seize glory for himself."

"Isn't it possible for someone to humbly offer trivial information that clutters the sermon, but sincerely mistake the Lord's leading in it?"

"That happens all the time, especially among beginners. The key is to constantly question whether the data before you will help the vehicle to reach its destination. Trivia are like sidetracks."

Paul stopped writing to ask another question, but he caught Dr. Vickerson staring out the window. There was a deep sadness in his eyes.

"Dr. Vickerson?"

His voice awakened the old man from his distant thoughts.

"Excuse me. Where was I"

"You were discussing the importance of scholarship."

---

*Experience the exhilaration that
comes from discovering the deep,
hidden treasures of God's Word,
treasures that cannot be
unearthed by a half-hearted effort
using a child's toy shovel.*

"Oh, yes." The old man shook his head at himself, then continued.

"The godly use of scholarship opens new windows of understanding for people to see their great God, while an ungodly use of it serves more to showcase the preacher's own learning. Praise be to King Ego instead of King Jesus.

"That is why scholarship alone will not fill the reservoir. It also takes great prayer to do so. Somewhere in this little notebook I have included a quote from E.M. Bounds in his classic work on prayer. Ah, here it is."

Dr. Vickerson found the page he was searching for and began to read:

> We have emphasized sermon preparation
> until we have lost sight of the important thing
> to be prepared—the heart. A prepared heart is
> much better than a prepared sermon. A pre-
> pared heart will make a prepared sermon.

Again he went through his ritual of carefully closing the ragged booklet and returning it to its place on the table.

"It is easy to use techniques of preaching in a mechanistic way, manipulating them for self-advancement rather than the advancement of God's kingdom. Bounds reminds us of the importance of a prepared heart."

"How would I pray to properly prepare my heart for preaching?" Paul asked. "I want my motives for attaining excellence to be pure, but I admit that self often gets in the way."

"Self often gets in the way of even the most godly ministers, but let me give you a few ideas on how to overcome that problem."

Dr. Vickerson stopped momentarily. He rubbed his eyes again and after collecting his thoughts proceeded.

"Have you tried devoting one whole day out of each month entirely to prayer? Nothing will fill you more with the sense of God's strength and presence than long, uninterrupted periods of prayer. Take a walk out into a lonely place like Jesus did. Get alone with God. And if possible, pray out loud. I have found that praying aloud here in my apartment keeps my mind from drifting and helps me better pour out my heart before the Lord."

"What kinds of things should I pray about in those times?"

"Take a list of your members and pray through the list, concentrating on what you know of their needs. Pray for the spiritual leadership of your church. Pray for your family and for yourself. Pray for vision and wisdom to lead God's people. You need to be alone with God before you can effectively usher others into His presence.

"In addition to a monthly day of prayer, a personal 'midweek prayer meeting' is crucial."

"What do you mean by 'midweek prayer meeting'?" Paul asked as he wrote the phrase in his notes.

"Often we spend so much time gathering information in our studies that we never stop to pray over it. We plunge headlong into our sermon outlines without seeking the Lord's guidance on how to handle the materials before us.

"So schedule time to pray in the middle of the week. Take the information you have gleaned for Sunday's sermon and pray about it. Pray about the present makeup and mood of your congregation. Think of how a specific young person, a single adult, a divorcee, an elderly widow, a person who is unemployed, or one who is suffering from a terminal disease might react to your message. Ask the Spirit of God to help you to take the materials you have gathered and bring them to bear upon the congregation's life and needs."

"I know of some preachers who sit in the pews where their people sit and pray for their needs," Paul commented.

"That is a good practice, but make sure you add to it the element of next Sunday's sermon. We often make the mistake of separating our prayers for the people from our ministry of the Word to those people. How should the message be shaped to show a sensitivity to their needs?

"This kind of prayer brings an added dimension to preaching. I think this is what the apostles were getting at in Acts 6 when they linked prayer together with the ministry of the Word as their two major responsibilities before God.

"You must be sure to wait on God. How few preachers really wait on God when it comes to Sunday's message! Then after your personal 'midweek prayer meeting' you can fine-tune your message accordingly, allowing it to draw from the reservoir of living waters which the Holy Spirit is filling up within you."

"Those are excellent suggestions, Dr. Vickerson. I intend to hold my first 'midweek prayer meeting' this Wednesday."

"Without such prayer efforts, your sermon becomes a testimony to your trust in self instead of your reliance on God's faithfulness. The one glorifies *you* while the other exalts God. You should feel naked if you step into the pulpit without clothing yourself in prayer. In fact you *are* naked without it.

"Paul, I know you have prayed fervently for your people before, but my focus here is on linking prayer more closely to the purpose and direction of your preaching and ministry of the Word. And there is one other area of prayer that is vitally important. It also concerns your motives and your heart."

"What's that?" Paul's curiosity was aroused.

"Your fellow preachers need your prayers. How often do you pray for their ministries? You need to be as earnest for their work as you are for your own."

"I can hardly find the time to pray for myself as I should, yet you're saying that praying for other pastors is an important key to keeping my own motives pure?"

"Absolutely. Ask yourself if you can genuinely rejoice with those who rejoice and weep with those who weep when it comes to their successes and failures in the pastorate. Because of our sinful natures we tend toward the very opposite. We gloat over others' failures and grit our teeth begrudgingly at their successes."

"I know I should pray more for others, and I know exactly what you mean about motives, but I find it hard to pray sincerely for someone else when my own ministry is so faltering."

"Pray even when you don't feel like it. The Lord will honor your struggles at honest and faithful prayer. He will lead you into the liberating experience of rejoicing when others achieve more visible success than yourself."

"You sound like you're speaking from experience, Dr. Vickerson."

"Professional jealousies are just as prevalent on the seminary level as they are in the pastorate and every other walk of life. The only way I have ever learned to overcome them is through a discipline that includes heavy doses of prayer for my colleagues."

"That's amazing! Seminary professors are human after all!"

Dr. Vickerson managed a faint smile at Paul's remark, more out of politeness than anything else. The grief that enshrouded him left little room for humor this morning. Quickly he returned to the business at hand.

"The third way you fill the reservoir is through personal Bible study that goes beyond your immediate ministry needs. This will also help you test your motives and search your heart.

"Those who only study what they teach must question their own love for God's Word. But if you devour whole portions of Scripture for your own edification and out of your own great love for the Bible, you will sense confirmation within your spirit that your heart is right before God. How few preachers truly love the Scriptures!

"G. Campbell Morgan made it his practice each Saturday to read one whole book of the Bible, one not directly related to Sunday's sermon. When he entered the pulpit the following morning he was full of the Word of God. Morgan also noted how often the Spirit of God would cause him to draw directly from the Scriptures he had read the day before, even though he had not intended to. His message was bathed in Scripture as well as in prayer and scholarship.

"Read the sermons of the Reformers like Calvin, Luther, and Latimer, and you will see the great reservoir of Scripture in their messages. You have been studying some of their messages lately, haven't you, Paul?"

"Yes, I have. In fact, I chose to study Latimer first because I had never read any of his sermons before. He was an amazing preacher!"

"Yes, but notice the depth of biblical language in those sermons—not just the direct quotes, but all the scriptural allusions."

Dr. Vickerson sat back, sighed deeply, then began to summarize.

"When you put the three together—scholarship, prayer, and Bible study—you begin to experience what is called 'unction,' which is the Spirit of God working mightily in and through you as you preach. Spurgeon said that no one knows exactly what unction is, but the people can tell if the man in the pulpit has it or not.

"You will have filled the reservoir to overflowing, and it will come spilling forth as from the fount of living waters on Sunday morning. Your people will see the difference. It is the difference between one slightly brushed by the Spirit and one fully possessed by the power of God.

"That, my son, is the difference between the reservoir and the water pipe. When you offer your seminar on preaching, don't fail to emphasize Reservoir Power. It is the most crucial of all ingredients, for by it the preacher *himself* is prepared, and not just the message.

"And with that I think I'll stop for the day. Lord willing, I'll be in better spirits again by next week. Can you show yourself to the door, Paul?"

"Sure. I'll lock the door on the way out. Dr. Vickerson, I'll be praying for you this week. If you need me, please call."

"Thank you, Paul. It helps to know that."

As the old man slowly made his way toward his bedroom door Paul watched momentarily before leaving the apartment. He had come in such high spirits, but now a heaviness gripped his own heart, a heaviness that would remain throughout the week before him.

18

A Visit to Forest Hills

By Thursday Paul could wait no longer; concern for his beloved mentor had burdened him all week. Over lunch Susan encouraged him to spend the afternoon with Dr. Vickerson. Meanwhile she planned to take James and John shopping.

"I can't believe how organized you are!" Paul exclaimed. "School doesn't start for another month yet."

"The secret is to start early," she replied. "The malls are advertising big back-to-school sales this week, and the early bird catches the worm!"

"That's the perfect aphorism for shopping—shopping's for the birds!" Paul retorted.

"You and your aphorisms. Ever since Dr. Vickerson told you about aphorisms that's all I hear! Aphorisms!

Aphorisms! Aphorisms!" Susan replied, pretending to be irritated.

"You and your sales! That's all I hear. Sales! Sales! Sales!" Paul laughed as he kissed her goodbye.

As he pulled out of the driveway Susan's comment about starting early popped into his mind. Good preaching isn't the only thing that benefits from an early start; good homemaking does too.

Dr. Vickerson's face lit up when Paul appeared at his door.

"Paul, I can't believe you're here. I was thinking about you this very moment."

"Well, I've been thinking about you all week. How are you doing, Dr. Vickerson?"

"I'm feeling better today, thank you. Especially since you're here. I apologize for being so moody last Monday. I'm afraid I was a little snappy."

"No need to apologize. You've been through a rough time."

"Paul, listen. Could I impose upon you for a big favor?"

"Just name it."

"Could you drive me out to Forest Hills Cemetery? I hate to ask, but I have the strongest desire to visit Emily's grave."

"But I thought she died in Florida."

"She did, but years ago we purchased cemetery lots near her parents' graves. We agreed to use our lots even after we moved away. I'm sorry to impose upon you. It's about a 30-minute ride to the cemetery; I'll pay for the gas."

"I'm willing to take you, and forget about the gas, but are you sure you want to go?"

"I'm sure. Visiting Emily's grave will be good therapy."

In the car Dr. Vickerson reminisced how he first met Emily. He told about their courtship days and the wedding ceremony at Parson Pearson's manse. "Parson Percy Pearson! What a tongue-twister!" His mood seemed much better, although his voice betrayed some sadness.

When they pulled into Forest Hills Cemetery Dr. Vickerson stopped reminiscing and directed Paul to the gravesite.

"What is your only comfort, in life and in death?" he asked as the car slowed to a stop near Emily Vickerson's marker.

Paul was about to respond, but before he could open his mouth Dr. Vickerson continued:

> That I belong—body and soul, in life and in death—not to myself but to my faithful Savior, Jesus Christ, who at the cost of His own blood has fully paid for all my sins and has completely freed me from the dominion of the devil; that He protects me so well that without the will of my Father in heaven not a hair can fall from my head; indeed, that everything must fit His purpose for my salvation. Therefore, by His Holy Spirit, He also assures me of eternal life, and makes me wholeheartedly willing and ready from now on to live for Him.

"Heidelberg Catechism, Question 1." Dr. Vickerson said, turning to Paul. "And how does the other half live without that assurance? Emily cannot come back to be with me, but someday soon I will finish my course here on earth. I will see my Savior, and I will see my wife!"

Dr. Vickerson pulled a yellowed, wrinkled handkerchief from his front coat pocket. He smiled weakly and said, "I'm sorry for acting this way. Do you mind if I spend a little time alone, Paul?"

"Of course not," Paul said softly.

He excused himself and began walking in the direction of the large brick church adjacent to the cemetery, leaving the old man at his wife's grave. He stopped under a giant oak tree near the front steps of the church. From that vantage point he could see Dr. Vickerson leaning on his cane near Emily's grave. He appeared to be speaking aloud, but Paul couldn't hear his voice. From time to time the professor paused to wipe his eyes with his handkerchief. Paul had to chuckle a little at the handkerchief. It looked as old as the professor himself.

As he looked on quietly in the cool of the tall shade tree, a voice from behind startled him: "May I help you with something?"

Turning, he observed a kindly gray-haired gentleman who was obviously the church custodian standing there with two bulging trashbags, one in each hand.

"Oh, I didn't see you. I'm just waiting for my friend." Paul nodded in the direction of Dr. Vickerson. "But since you ask, I was wondering who your pastor is. I don't see a name on the bulletin board."

"We don't have a preacher right now. Last one left about four months ago."

"So your pulpit is vacant. Who was your last minister?"

"Reverend Scott. Laird Scott. Do you know him?"

"No, I don't think so. Do you know why he left?"

"Well, I guess he got tired of us and we got tired of him," the custodian said with a nervous laugh. "When he first came he was a real ball of fire. Fresh out of seminary, mind you. But after a few years he just plain ran out of gas. People began to fuss about his preaching; some even stopped coming to church—said they wouldn't be back until he left. I guess after three or four years' preaching in the same place there's not much left to be said. Finally the pressure got so great he just quit."

"Where did he go?" Paul asked.

"He took a job in his wife's hometown, working in her father's hardware store. Plans to take it over after his father-in-law retires."

"So he left the ministry altogether?" Paul sighed.

"Last thing he said as he cleared out his study was, 'I don't care if I never preach another sermon.' He sold all his books—every last one."

Paul shook his head. "Probably to some eager young seminary student."

"How'd you guess that? You're absolutely right."

Out of the corner of his eye Paul could see Dr. Vickerson starting back toward the car. "I see my friend is ready, so I better go. Nice talking to you."

"Same to you. Have a good day."

Paul managed to smile as he thought to himself, "Sure, have a good day. Another preacher bites the dust—so have a good day."

19

The Three R's of Preaching

Back in the car Dr. Vickerson seemed relieved; it was obvious that a burden had been lifted. But the conversation with the custodian depressed Paul. It reminded him of a thought that had been hounding him lately.

"Dr. Vickerson, maybe it's time for me to go to a new congregation."

"Oh, why's that?"

"I know my preaching has improved and will continue to improve. I'm determined about that. But I've been with the same people since I graduated from seminary. They're the only congregation I've ever known. I'm the only pastor many of them have had. I'm running out of new things to say. I'm starting to repeat myself."

He paused, then added, "Maybe they need a new voice, someone with new ideas, a fresh approach. Maybe I should step aside so they can move on in the Lord."

"I appreciate your struggle, Paul. I've heard your sentiments expressed many times before, but I believe such thinking is fallacious."

"What's wrong with it? It seems to make sense."

"First, what new teaching can a new preacher add? If it's new, is it sound? If it's good theology, why didn't the former pastor teach it?"

"Maybe he never learned it himself," Paul suggested.

"If he didn't, why not? Did he stop learning after graduation? Was there no pressing on to know the Lord?"

"Perhaps the duties of the pastorate bogged him down. He couldn't find time to study and keep growing."

"Now we're back to priorities. If that's the case, he needs to change his lifestyle. Unfortunately, some think the only way out is to change pastorates or even quit the ministry."

"Like Laird Scott," Paul muttered to himself.

"Much of the work of ministry is reminding. In fact, when we get back to my apartment I want you to make a note about the three R's of preaching."

"You must have heard Susan talking about shopping for school today," Paul laughed. "What are the three R's of preaching?"

"The first stands for *reminding*," Dr. Vickerson said. "As I said, most of your ministry is reminding. The apostle Paul declared to the Ephesians that in three years' time he had taught them the whole counsel of God."

"Yes, and then he moved on from there," Paul added.

"But he moved because of his calling as an apostle to the Gentiles. Paul was always pressing on to establish new works. He was a church planter, not a pastor.

"At some point in your ministry you naturally begin to repeat yourself. But there is nothing wrong with reminding people, just so you do so in fresh ways. The apostle said in Philippians 3:1, 'To write the same things again is no trouble to me, and it is a safeguard for you." He saw the importance of reminding.

"Paul, haven't you ever read a familiar passage, only to realize you had failed to apply its truth to your daily walk?"

"Sure. Lately the book of Jonah has done that. I know the importance of reaching the lost, but Jonah reminded me to get back to it. I had lost my sense of urgency."

"That's exactly what I'm talking about. That happens throughout your life. Familiar passages become fresh all over again. Think of how Jesus exhorted the church at Ephesus to return to their first love. In fact, young man, when you get to be my age most everything you hear is reminding! If I had to hear something new in order for each week's sermon to be of value to me there would be little need to attend."

> *Most of your ministry is reminding. There is nothing wrong with reminding people, just so you do so in fresh ways.*

"That bothers me, though. I have an elderly woman in my church who knows far more Bible than I do. I wonder why she listens to my preaching at all. She should be teaching me instead."

"She needs you to remind her through your preaching. What did the apostle say to the Colossians? 'As you therefore have received Christ Jesus the Lord, so walk in Him.' Each week she must feed on God's Word; it is her spiritual food. Just because you eat fresh bread this week, that doesn't mean you won't do so again!"

"Yes, but if this Sunday's message is the same as last Sunday's, the people wouldn't be so happy. It's not exactly like eating another slice of fresh bread."

"Yes and no. When bread is served fresh and hot, baked with fine, rich ingredients in an oven tempered by years of baking, it is a delightful experience—the kind you want to have again and again. Serve your sermon up fresh and hot. Bread of heaven, fresh from the pastor's oven! Mmmm, I can smell it now!"

"But I better change the message from week to week."

"Yes, but each message will contain elements that remind. For the older saints everything about the message may only serve as a reminder. What makes the difference is *how you prepare and serve those reminders*. For example, you might preach the same sermon but use all new illustrations. Serve the old truth in a new dish. It's like having scalloped potatoes one week and mashed the next."

"You're making me hungry! I understand what you mean; in fact, I'm also hungry to try it out! So the first R stands for reminding. What is the second R?"

"The second R is for *repetition*. By repeating I mean a word-for-word repetition of a theme or idea. You might repeat the identical line several times throughout the message."

"I can think of a good example," Paul replied: "Martin Luther King's famous 'I Have a Dream' sermon."

"Yes. In that message he kept repeating that theme throughout. You may not remember every single idea he expressed, but his overpowering theme is fixed in your memory."

"But usually when I think of repetition, I think of something negative. People often complain that the minister keeps repeating himself."

"You're right. A lot of repetition is unnecessary. But purposeful, well-prepared repetition is very effective. Poor repetition is often a sign of poor preparation, but I'm thinking of repetition which is thought-out and deliberate."

"What makes for good, well-prepared repetition?" Paul asked as he slowed for a red light.

"An excellent question. Good repetition consists of three key elements. First, a theme that is worth repeating; second, strong supporting materials sandwiched between each repetition; and third, a strategic ordering of those materials so that each idea builds on the one before it, expanding on it and leading the sermon to a strong conclusion. Don't make the mistake of deflating the buildup of the message. That results in an anticlimactic ending. Save the most powerful and fitting illustration for the grand finale."

"So I get a strong theme and gather supporting materials, then order them in a way that builds to the strongest conclusion. Any scriptural examples of repetition?" Paul asked.

"When Jesus pronounced woe upon the Pharisees in Matthew 23, or was it chapter 24? No, I think 23," Dr. Vickerson said, shaking his head in frustration over his uncertainty, a factor he attributed to old age.

"Anyway, Jesus repeated 'Woe to you, scribes, Pharisees, hypocrites!' several times. His final woe, when He described them as children of those who killed the prophets and how their hands were guilty of shedding the blood of the righteous, was the most powerful one of all. If you study that sermon you'll see all three principles at work: strong theme, strong supporting evidences with a strong ordering of that evidence, and finally a strong conclusion.

"Remember E. V. Hill's Good Friday message?"

"Do you mean, 'It's Friday, But Sunday's Coming?'" Paul asked.

"Yes, that's it—a perfect example of the power of repetition."

"I think the great power of that message was in the theme itself. It makes the resurrection so vivid."

"Yes, the theme must be strong for repetition to work well. Pity the congregation that must endure a message that keeps repeating a poor theme! Incidentally, repetition is another one of those *vehicles* we talked about. It's a powerful way to transport your sermon to its *destination*."

Dr. Vickerson hurried to conclude when he realized that Paul was turning onto the street leading to the apartment building. "The third R stands for *reiterating*. By reiteration I mean repetition that takes place within a thought—not a word-for-word repetition of a theme, but a repeating.in other words. You might repeat the same idea two or three times within the same paragraph, but in different words."

"Is that because someone might miss the idea if you only say it once?"

"Yes, or some people may not grasp the full meaning of your thought if you only say it one way. Perhaps it's not clear enough to them, as when you use an unfamiliar term that confuses or misleads them.

"Before the invention of the printing press people understood and used the techniques of oral communication far better than we do today," Dr. Vickerson explained. "Few could read or write. News and ideas were transmitted largely by word of mouth. People weren't able to go back and read over what they missed upon first hearing. So reiteration was an important technique to help them remember."

"Does the Bible use this method? After all, many people in Bible times couldn't read either."

"The Bible is full of reiteration. Look at Hebrew poetry; so much is in couplet form. That fact even helps you memorize Scripture. Let me demonstrate what I mean. Isaiah 53 describes the Suffering Servant through the use of several couplets. 'He was wounded for our transgressions' is coupled with 'He was bruised for our iniquities.'

" 'All we like sheep have gone astray' goes with 'we have each one turned his own way,' " Paul recited as he picked up on the idea.

"Very good. Jesus did the same. That's one reason why it's so easy to remember His sayings." Dr. Vickerson began another example. "No man can serve two masters; either he will hate the one and love the other. . . ."

He paused for Paul to complete: ". . . or else he will hold to the one and despise the other."

"You get the point."

"Yes. Reiteration helps the audience hear and remember truth by restating it in different ways," Paul summarized.

"One type of reiteration you shouldn't forget is the sermon illustration. It repeats an idea in an interesting way without tiring the people. It illustrates that point, shedding light on it."

Then Dr. Vickerson had an afterthought: "Like repetition, reiteration can also be done poorly. Some preachers use it as filler while trying to remember their next point. One of my colleagues made a habit of repeating his previous statement while he scanned his notes to find his next point."

"Sounds annoying," Paul said.

"It was very irritating, and it gave the people too much time to sit and wait. They lost attention through his poor use of reiteration. Repetition or reiteration that is not purposeful and well-prepared weakens the message. Don't let these techniques fool you, Paul. They seem simple, but using them effectively can be tricky. To repeat something I told you when we first began to meet, the key to fresh preaching is *agony and hard work*. The same is true here."

"You like to *repeat* that a lot, Dr. Vickerson!" Paul teased as he turned off the engine.

"Yes, but it's *purposeful* and *deliberate* repetition," the professor laughed.

"So you really think it's possible to stay with the same congregation for many years and still do a good job?" Paul asked, returning to what had started the whole conversation.

"It's not only possible, but most of the effective and successful pulpit ministries involve men who have stayed for many years in one place—people like Martin Lloyd Jones, Charles Spurgeon, and a host of others.

"I almost forgot!" exclaimed Dr. Vickerson. He reached inside his coat, pulled out a large white business envelope, and handed it to Paul.

"What's this?" Paul asked.

"It's your homework assignment."

"Homework assignment?"

"I'm going to visit my sister for a few weeks."

"That's great! That's just the medicine you need right now."

"I guess she could tell over the phone the other day that I was pretty low. I thought I'd better give you some homework to do while I'm away. I intended to mail this to you, but since you surprised me with your visit I'll give it to you now and save the postage."

"When are you planning to go?"

"I'm leaving in the morning by bus. I was going to call you tonight because I know you wouldn't have received the letter before Monday. Actually there's a little more to it than all of this, though. . . ."

"Dr. Vickerson, I can't believe how well this is working out," Paul interrupted. "My family is leaving for vacation next week, but I didn't want to tell you until Monday. I thought it might further discourage you at this time."

"Where are you going?"

"The great Northwest! For the whole month of August!"

"I note a hint of excitement in your voice. The Northwest is beautiful country. Whatever you do, don't miss Paradise!"

"Paradise?"

"That's the name of the Visitor Center on Mount Rainier. And believe me, it almost lives up to its name! Listen, one of the assignments I've given you has to do with illustrations. Vacation is an excellent time to find new illustrations. Be sure to keep a notebook with you and write down every idea. Don't rely on your memory, or by the time you come home you'll forget a lot.

"And don't try to come up with a list of 'Ripley's Believe It Or Not' stories. Those thick volumes of sermon illustrations tend to be filled with that junk. Look for material in the ordinary things of life. After all, that's what Jesus did. He used examples such as salt and light, sand and rock, lost sheep and a lost coin. By using those kinds of illustrations Jesus surrounded his audiences with everyday reminders of spiritual truth.

"Just listen to me. I never stop, do I, Paul?"

"That's fine, Dr. Vickerson. I could listen to you all day long. Besides, I think I'm the one who interrupted you a few minutes ago. You started to say that there was more to your trip than 'all this.' What were you going to tell me?"

"Oh, it wasn't anything important—just that I had already planned to visit my sister in a few weeks, but when she heard how discouraged I sounded over the phone she insisted I come out right away. So I called the bus station to find out the best time to travel, and now everything's all arranged for tomorrow.

"You better get going now, son. I know Susan will be waiting for you, and I have some final packing to do. Call me when you get back!"

"We'll drop you a postcard—one of those 'wish you were here' types!"

"Great! Now don't forget that envelope. You might have a chance to get some work done before we meet again. But don't ruin your vacation with too much church work."

"I'll try not to!" Paul laughed.

"I'll see you in September, Lord willing."

"You too. Have a good time at your sister's. And Dr. Vickerson, thanks again for all your help and time. It has meant so much to me. You've saved my ministry, you know."

"No, Paul. You've been called by God, and by His grace you'll never turn back. More than anything you've helped me through a lonely and difficult time. I don't know what I would have done without you, my friend."

The two shook hands warmly, and then the old professor placed his hand gently on Paul's shoulder. For a moment he searched Paul's eyes in order to gain his fullest attention. Then he spoke:

"Son, do you remember the most often-repeated command in the Holy Scriptures?"

Paul stopped to think, but before he could speak Dr. Vickerson answered his own question.

"'Fear not.' The words 'fear not' or 'be not afraid' or something to that effect appear more in the Bible than any other command that God gives His children."

Paul nodded in agreement as the professor continued.

"From time to time I've sensed a great deal of fear in you. Fear that your people might reject you. Fear that you might fail in your calling. Maybe even fear that the Lord will let you down?"

Dr. Vickerson's eyes were full of love for the young pastor as he fixed his gaze on Paul.

"No, son, I didn't save your ministry. You have a great God Who loves you more dearly than you love yourself. He began a good work in you and He will not stop until He has completed it. He called you to this difficult work, but He has also promised to equip you for it and to never leave you or forsake you along the way. If I have been of help to you, praise God for His provision. And remember, if God provided for your needs at this crisis time in your ministry, He will do it again. Fear not, Paul. Always remember that your God will not let you down."

With that the old man warmly embraced Paul, then turned toward the apartment building. Paul watched as Dr. Vickerson slowly made his way to the building entrance. At the door he turned, smiled, waved a final goodbye, then disappeared inside.

20

The Sixfold Path

The station wagon was packed full, inside and out. The carrier on the luggage rack was stuffed with camping equipment: tent, sleeping bags, cooking utensils, air mattresses, stove and lantern, axe for chopping firewood—even winter clothing and raingear in case of severe weather in the higher elevations.

The Andrews left home shortly after 4:00 A.M. Susan and the boys slept while Paul drove through the early-morning darkness. As he drove, he brooded. Even the spectacular morning sunrise did little to brighten his discouraged spirit. It was almost eight before Susan began to stir.

"I'm so tired from all the packing and getting ready," she yawned. "I need this vacation!"

"I appreciate this station wagon. It's so quiet and smooth compared to that old clunker I use for work," Paul said somewhat grimly. "I'm enjoying the peaceful ride with those two sleeping back there."

"Are you sure you're enjoying it? Seems to me like you're upset about something."

"What do you mean by that?" Paul asked defensively.

"I've been married to you long enough to know when you're in a bad mood. What's bothering you, anyway?"

"I can't believe Tom Fedderhoffer!" Paul exploded.

"Quiet!" Susan whispered. "You'll wake the children."

"I lined up speakers for each Sunday while I'm gone," Paul said with lowered voice. "Then Tom waltzes into the office after church yesterday with a big gleam in his eyes, and he announces to me that Dr. Mackey is filling the pulpit while I'm gone."

"Dr. Mackey's preaching? Paul, how can that be? What about the ministers you lined up?"

"That's what I asked Tom. He said he had approached each member of the Church Board before worship and got their 'enthusiastic' approval.

"I'm angry the Board let Tom get away with it. They specifically instructed me to find my replacements. I wouldn't be surprised at all to find out Dr. Mackey has become my *permanent* replacement by the time we get back home!"

"You're not serious, are you, Paul? They couldn't do that, could they?" Susan sat up straight in her seat. A look of alarm swept over her face.

"I don't know if they could, but they decided to have him come behind my back. Who knows what else they might do! After all, Dr. Mackey announced recently that he's retiring from his heavy evangelistic service schedule. He said he wouldn't mind finding a vacant church near his home to serve as an interim pastor. Tom Fedderhoffer idolizes that man so much. He might try anything to get him to take over Calvary Church."

"Oh, no," Susan gasped, then began to cry. "Paul, why in the world are we going on vacation if we don't even know you'll have a job when we get back home?"

"What was I supposed to do? Come home after church and tell you everything's off? I didn't know this was going to happen! Besides, what could I do? Tell the Church Board I changed my mind? Tell them I wouldn't be taking my vacation after all? 'Cancel Dr. Mackey—I've decided to stay home! I feel so dedicated to Calvary Church that I don't even want a vacation this year!'"

Paul shouted his last two remarks so loudly that he woke up the children. James yawned and stretched as John rubbed the sleepers out of his eyes.

"What's wrong, mom?" asked James. "Why are you crying? Do we have to turn around and go home?"

"I don't know, honey. Mommy's all right. Listen, are you two getting hungry yet?" Susan asked, changing the subject.

"Yeah!" said John. "Can we get pancakes for breakfast?"

"Of course." Susan tried to sound cheery. "Pancakes for breakfast is our vacation tradition."

"I can't wait till dad cooks that Canadian bacon when we're camped up in the mountains!" cried James. "Are you gonna get some Canadian bacon for us this year, dad?"

"Sure I am," Paul managed a smile.

"Great!" shouted James and John.

"Listen, Susan," Paul said as he took an exit from the interstate to find a restaurant. "There's nothing we can do about our situation back home. I don't know what's going to happen there, but we can't turn around and go back now. This all came up so suddenly yesterday. What do we do, go home and attend church while Dr. Mackey preaches?"

Susan sat in silence with her head turned toward the side window to hide her tears from the children. After Paul parked the car, the kids jumped out and raced to the restaurant door to find a table, leaving Paul and Susan alone in the car.

"Go ahead in and order without me, Paul," she sobbed. "I don't have much of an appetite right now."

"Okay," Paul said with resignation. He took the keys from the ignition and opened his door.

"This is just great, Paul Andrews! What a wonderful way to start our vacation!" Susan cried out. Then she mocked Paul's voice to the children: 'Let's go on vacation, James and John. We'll have a great time. We'll cook Canadian bacon in the mountains. We'll go visit Mount Rushmore to see the presidents' faces. We'll check out Mount Rainier. Then when we get back home, we'll see if I still have a job!' "

"I'm sorry, honey. You have a right to be angry with me," Paul replied quietly.

"Just go and leave me alone. The kids are waiting for you! Tell them I'm not feeling well enough to eat right now."

After breakfast Paul found Susan standing with her back to him at the edge of the parking lot. He was surprised to find that she was actually smiling a little when he reached her side.

"We'll be okay, Paul," she said more calmly. "All this had to happen for a reason. I don't know what the reason is, but you're right—there's nothing we could do about the situation back home. Even if we turned around right now, there's nothing we could really do about it. Somehow or other you and I have to forget about the church for awhile and enjoy our time with the kids."

She glanced over her shoulder at James and John, who were throwing catch in the parking lot. She flinched to see James throw a wild pitch that hit the pavement and bounced off the bumper of a car.

"Be careful, boys!" she shouted. "You break something and you'll pay for it!

"Look at those two little *angels* of ours!" she said to Paul. "They're growing up so fast."

"A few more years and they'll be off to college," Paul sighed.

"That's why we have to enjoy ourselves on this vacation. This is the one time out of the whole year that we're all together as a family. We can't allow the church to take this time away from us."

"Lord knows, they take enough time already," Paul sighed again.

"I'm up for driving now, so we better go."

"Are you sure you're not too tired to drive?" Paul asked. "After all, you've really been working hard to get ready for the trip."

"Oh, I'm awake, all right. *Wide awake!*" Susan laughed.

While Susan drove, James and John entertained themselves with the new pocket video games she had bought them. She had planned a wide assortment of little surprises to help the boys pass the time on the long trip. Meanwhile, Paul attempted to finish a book that Dr. Vickerson had assigned him.

"What are you reading?" Susan asked.

"A book on sermon illustrations. I stopped by the library after my visit with Dr. Vickerson. I knew I wouldn't get back there before vacation, so I read a few articles and picked up the books he recommended."

"Any good illustrations in it?"

"A few, but this isn't a collection of illustrations. It's a book *about* illustrations—where to find them, how to collect and store them, how to tailor them to the sermon, dangers to avoid—things like that."

"I hope you're not planning to read a lot this vacation. I would like to have my husband with me."

"I promise not to study much. Dr. Vickerson wants me to keep a notebook of illustrations I find in our travels, so I wanted to finish this book before we left home."

"How far did you get?"

"I have less than a hundred pages to go."

"Has it been any help?" Susan feigned a yawn.

"You just want me to talk to you while you're driving," Paul said.

"Why do you say that?"

"I know my wife pretty well by now," Paul answered.

"Well, If you're not going to sleep so you'll be ready to drive again, then yes. I'd rather you talk to me than read a book. What do you need to learn about sermon illustrations, anyway?"

"What do you mean by that?"

"It seems pretty simple to me: You prepare a sermon, then you throw in a few good illustrations to keep your people awake and help them remember the main points. Everybody knows that having good illustrations is the most important part of the sermon. When the people go home they forget the sermon, but they remember the illustrations. There! I've explained everything about illustrations to you, so put your book away and talk to me. I can teach you more than that book!"

"Well, my dear expert," Paul said sarcastically, "If you know so much, then tell me what the word means."

"What word?"

"*Illustrate*. What does *illustrate* mean?"

"I don't know—to tell a story about something," Susan guessed halfheartedly.

"Wrong. It means 'to shed light on, to make bright, to adorn, to make clear.' An illustration is an example or a story that helps to shed light on or clarify a truth."

"That's what I just said, 'to tell a story about something,'" Susan needled. Then she added, "Now I'll give you a good illustration for your notebook. You can use this in a sermon on the family."

"What's that?" Paul asked a little impatiently.

"Husbands, love your wives. When you go on vacations with your families, don't take your work with you. Because then it isn't a vacation after all, is it? I knew a man once—a preacher, in fact—" Susan said in a mock pulpit voice, "who took a stack of books about preaching on vacation. He neglected his wife and children. His vacation was no vacation at all! So husbands, love your wives and your children, too. Leave your work at home! There—write that one down in your notebook."

"Very funny. Listen, I told you I have less than a hundred pages. After I finish, I won't start any more books."

"Is that a promise?"

"That's a promise. Remember, I'm a minister, and ministers never lie."

"What about that stack of books I saw you pack in your briefcase?"

"I brought those in order to start the 'sixfold path of reading.' But I'll wait till I get home."

" 'The sixfold path of reading'?" Susan laughed. "What on earth is that?"

"It's a way of reading books. It was in one of Dr. Vickerson's assignments."

"Oh, this is getting better. First you read about illustrations. Then you read a book on how to read books! By the way, how did you find time to read all this last Thursday?"

"It was only one chapter. I studied three or four short chapters and articles, that's all."

"I won't even ask about the other articles, but I *am* curious about this sixfold path of reading."

"No, you're not."

"Yes, I am. I don't want to miss out on it. This might change my life!" Susan teased.

"Listen. Please let me read the rest of this. I won't study any more books till we get back home. Okay?"

"Okay," Susan smiled.

"Dad?"

"Yes, John." Paul sighed, knowing what was next.

"What's the sixfold path of reading?"

"Yeah, dad, I want to know too!" James chimed in.

"Susan, watch where you're driving!" Paul shouted. The car had suddenly swerved off the road onto the shoulder, then back again.

"I'm sorry. I can't help it!" Susan laughed uncontrollably. "Paul, tell us what the sixfold path of reading is! We're dying to know."

164

"We'll all be dead if you keep driving like that!" Paul snapped. "Instead of reading one book at a time, you read six at a time. You choose five books in five different categories—categories such as novels, historical books, biographicals, diaries and journals, and poetry. Then you choose one other in any area of personal interest. You read in all six at the same time so you're exposed to a wide variety of ideas instead of limiting yourself to one book. You gather sermon illustrations from all those different categories, thus ensuring greater variety in your preaching. That's the sixfold path of reading! Now is everybody happy?"

"Yes, except for one thing," Susan said, trying to keep a straight face.

"I'm afraid to ask. What's that?"

"If you're suppose to read six books at one time, where are your other five books? I only see one. And how do you read them all at once? Do you lay them all out side by side and go like this?" Susan opened her eyes as wide as she could and began jerking her head back and forth, pretending to scan six books at the same time.

"No, and watch you're driving. You're about to go off the road again!" Paul growled.

"Dad?"

"What, John? Here it comes again," Paul groaned.

"I think mom's right. Trying to read six books at the same time sounds really confusing," John said earnestly. "How *do* you do that?"

"This family!" Paul laughed. "I give up! It's going to be a long vacation." He took his book and stuffed it under the front floormat, then reached into the back seat for a pillow. "Maybe I'll get some sleep after all."

21

Turning the Light on the Sermon

The first long day of travel was coming to an end. The sun was setting, and Paul knew it would be dark before they reached their campground. He was glad to cover all those miles the first day, but everyone was tired by now.

"When are we stopping, dad?"

"In about 30 or 40 minutes."

"Dad?"

"What, James?"

"Are we going to build a campfire tonight?"

"Not tonight, James. We'll wait till we get to the national park before we do that."

"Boo! We want a campfire tonight!" John's reaction told Susan he was getting tired and crabby.

"I know you're disappointed, children," she soothed, "but we'll have lots of campfires before vacation is over.

Today was just a long travel day."

"It's a long way to Glacier National Park," Paul added. "We wanted to get as far as we could. You boys get some rest. We'll be stopping soon."

"So you managed to finish your book this afternoon. Boy, am I glad about that!" Susan was making conversation to help Paul keep awake. "Did you learn anything helpful from it?"

"Well, since you asked so nicely this time," Paul answered, "did you know that illustrations, like babies, have a habit of being born at awkward times?"

"I like that. That's pretty clever! Did you think that one up or was it in the book? If you thought it up I'm really impressed."

"No, I'm afraid it was in the book. But it points out a problem we preachers face in gathering illustrations. Often the examples pop up in the strangest places at the most inopportune times. You think to yourself, 'I have to write that down when I get home.' But by the time you get there you've forgotten. That's why Dr. Vickerson insisted that I get in the habit of carrying an illustration notebook with me everywhere I go."

"Even on vacation?"

"Especially on vacation! While I'm traveling I can concentrate more on observing the world around me. I'll see things I might have missed in the hectic pace back home."

"You better turn the headlights on. It's getting dark."

"This book stresses the importance of gathering illustrations all the time and saving them for just the right moment in just the right sermon," Paul said as he flicked on the lights.

"One mistake we often make is that we find a way to use a good illustration as soon as we hear it. We're too anxious to use it or we're afraid we'll forget it if we save it. Either way we end up forcing a great illustration into the sermon, even if it doesn't quite fit."

"I've heard you do that occasionally, especially after attending a Bible conference. You throw in all five or six of the best illustrations you heard that week whether they fit your message or not."

"Yes, and that confuses the congregation about the meaning of the message as well as robbing the illustration of its real potential."

"How fast are you going, Paul? Everyone's flicking their lights at you. There must be a state trooper up ahead."

"That's funny. It seems like they've been doing that ever since I turned my lights on. Do I have my high beams on by mistake?"

Paul flicked the dimmer switch, only to see his high beams come on, but they were shining way up in the air, missing the road altogether.

"I don't believe this. The back end of our car is so loaded down the high beams don't even hit the road. Everyone thinks they're on because the low beams are shining out so far."

Paul dimmed his lights again, but the oncoming traffic continued to signal.

"Do you think we ought to have them adjusted?" Susan asked. "It's a long trip, you know."

"Maybe, but right now get out my notebook!" Paul shouted as he turned on the map light. "Write this down for me."

"Write what down?" she asked, reaching for pen and pad.

"Write something about the headlights being out of adjustment so they don't light up the road. Just a few words to remind me. Tomorrow I'll fill in the details."

"You've been driving too long. What are you talking about?"

"Don't you see? This is a perfect illustration about illustrations. To illustrate means to shed light on. Our headlights are supposed to shed light on the highway, but they shine up into the air instead. They're totally ineffective!"

Susan gave Paul a blank look.

"Just like some illustrations that don't really shine any light on the subject they're supposed to."

"I still don't get it. How are you going to use this in a sermon? It sounds more like something for preachers."

"You're right. I'll use this when I talk to preachers about the dangers of illustrations. But I might be able to think of a way to use it in a sermon, too. Sometimes an event or idea stands out in your mind, so you write it down even if you aren't sure how to use it. Sooner or later something occurs."

"Okay, I've written it down, but I can't wait to see how you use this in a sermon.

Illustrations, like babies, have a habit of being born at awkward times. Get in the habit of carrying an illustration notebook.

"So what else did you learn about illustrations?" Susan wasn't that interested, but she knew it would keep Paul's mind from thinking how tired he was. In the back of her mind was Calvary Church and the situation with Dr. Mackey, but she intended to do her best to keep it from coming to the surface, especially late at night when they were both so tired.

"It's important to have a good system of collecting illustrations. I can't rely on coming up with just the right example or story each week. I need a stockpile to draw from."

"Why not just rely on those books of illustrations? You already have a couple in your study."

"They help a little, but most of the good stories are outdated and overused by now. The rest are usually so strange you have trouble believing they're true."

"I know what you mean. Some of those stories are so cornball!" Susan laughed. "And some are so old. I think if I hear about the farmer's barn burning down and those little chicks coming out from under the charred remains of their mother hen one more time..."

"Wait a minute," Paul interrupted. "Isn't this our exit?"

"No, we have a few more miles to go. Now tell me where you plan to find all these illustrations."

"Everywhere. The problem is that preachers wait until the last minute to look for them. By then it may be too late. That's what the book means about them being like babies, born at the wrong times."

"Like James deciding to be born on Easter Sunday! Remember how you panicked when my water broke two hours before Sunrise Service?"

"I finally got hold of that retired minister who came at the last minute. I don't think he appreciated being called at 5:00 A.M. Easter Sunday to fill the pulpit!" Paul laughed.

"But that's just the point," he continued. "Illustrations don't usually come to you; you have to go to them. So I want to try that 'sixfold path of reading' you made so much fun of this morning. I also intend to spend one day each month at the library looking through a stack of magazines. That will offer me a wide variety of sources. And I plan to keep this notebook with me to write down things as I observe them each day. I also plan to spend maybe five or ten minutes each day thinking up my own illustrations."

"You could look for illustrations in the objects you see around you," Susan suggested.

"Yes, Jesus used ordinary objects to illustrate divine truth—the hairs on our head, the birds of the air, the lilies of the field. Things people see again and again remind them of the truths He taught."

"So the key is to not wait until the last minute to find your materials. Then what do you do, review all your illustrations every so often in order to remind yourself what's available in the stockpile?"

"That's important, and also to review the list of the sermons I plan to preach during the next few months so I can be on the lookout ahead of time."

"Maybe you should put a list of the sermons on the inside cover of your Bible as a constant reminder," Susan suggested.

"That's a great idea! I think I'll do that. Thanks."

"Think nothing of it. I told you before that if you listened to me instead of reading all those books you might learn something."

"Another mistake we make is to choose an illustration too soon in our sermon preparation," Paul continued, pretending to ignore her last remark.

"That sounds like a contradiction to me. First you said ministers wait until it's too late to find their illustrations; now you say they start too early."

"What I mean is that if you decide too early to use a particular illustration, you might have trouble fitting it into the sermon. On the surface it looked all right, but after the sermon is constructed it really doesn't fit. Instead of forcing it into the message, it should be set aside for later."

"In other words, you should write your message first, then decide which illustrations best fit each point in it. I think that's fairly obvious."

"You're pretty smart!" Paul teased.

"Smart enough to tell you our exit is coming up in about two seconds."

"You're right. I almost drove past it."

Paul left the interstate and soon found the campground. He parked the station wagon strategically so it could shine light on their campsite. The car faced downhill into the campsite, so this time the high beams were just perfect for the occasion. While Paul and the boys struggled to put up the tent, Susan unloaded the sleeping bags and air mattresses.

"Well, we're on vacation!" Paul said, announcing the obvious as he crawled into his sleeping bag. "I think we need to thank the Lord for safe travel, for the car running so well, and for all the miles we got in."

The four bowed together and James prayed for Snooper. The beagle was spending the month at grandma's house.

John included Rusty and Rontu and Spot. The three gold-fish were staying next door at their neighbors' house.

Susan detected some anxiety and sadness in their prayers. "You don't need to worry about Snooper and the goldfish. They'll be just fine," she said soothingly.

"But, mom, what if they die?" John asked.

"Well, if the goldfish die we'll just go back to the pet store and buy new fish. This time we'll get some prettier fish—some of those beautiful-colored tropical fish. So don't worry about them, kids."

"Mom! Mom!" James reacted with amazement. "I don't believe you said that. How would you feel if I told dad, 'Don't worry if mom dies, you can just go out and get a new and prettier mom.' How would that make you feel?"

"Yeah, Mom!" Paul laughed. "How *would* you feel!"

Susan began laughing so hard that she lost control. Paul switched on the flashlight in time to see the tears streaming down her face. Her whole body, shaking inside her sleeping bag, created strange sound effects from her plastic air mattress.

"Why did you turn that light on? What are you doing? What are you looking for? Paul, where are you going?" Susan sputtered as Paul crawled out of his sleeping bag and began putting his pants on.

"I left my notebook in the car. I've got to write this one down! What a sermon illustration this will make!"

He unzipped the tent door and headed for the car. As he fumbled with the keys to unlock the car door he noticed the beautiful clear night sky. The stars seemed so near. They were shining so brightly this moonless summer night. The August air was warm and sweet.

"God, Your works are so magnificent. Your power is so great. Surely I can trust You to take care of Calvary Church while I'm out here on vacation."

Paul shook his head at himself, wondering why his faith was so small when his calling was so great.

22

Snob Appeal or Sense Appeal?

The third day out began with a stop at the Corn Palace in South Dakota. Paul dutifully took notes on the attraction, but back in the car he kept shaking his head about it.

"I can't believe we stopped early yesterday so we wouldn't miss this!" Susan groaned. "Who was it that told you this was a 'must see'?"

"Tim Foster," Paul mumbled under his breath.

"Tim Foster! The world's greatest time-waster! I should have guessed, but why did you listen to him?"

"I know. Big mistake. He told me we'd spend the whole day here. He said he browsed the hallways of the palace for hours."

"Hallways of the palace! Not my idea of a palace, Paul Andrews."

"I admit it's not everything I envisioned it to be. I guess there's a sermon illustration in this," Paul mused, "but for the life of me I don't know what it is. A building with cornstalks stuck on the outside of it. And to think they go to all that effort each year to redesign it!"

"It's just an ordinary building," Susan added. "I expected a real palace made of corn."

"You aren't the only one disappointed—look at James and John. Ice cream sandwiches at 9:30 in the morning don't even help.

"Oh, well, chalk it up to experience. Maybe someday I'll figure a way to use it in a sermon. Right now I'm drawing a blank."

"You and your sermon illustrations! I'll tell you how to use this in a sermon."

"How's that?"

"Think of the disappointment. After all the anticipation and the long miles to get here, what a letdown!"

"What are you trying to say?"

"Ask the congregation if they've ever made plans to go somewhere, expecting it to be very special, and then were disappointed when they discovered it was not what they imagined it would be. I'm sure everyone has had that kind of experience.

"Then you talk about going to heaven," Susan continued. "Ask the congregation something like 'Do you secretly fear that heaven isn't all it's cracked up to be? After all the wait and anticipation, are you afraid you'll be disappointed when you get there? Don't you ever wonder how God can entertain everyone for thousands and thousands of years, and they never get bored or let down?'"

"I see what you mean," Paul nodded. "That has possibilities."

"I even have the perfect question. You can ask them, 'Will those Ivory Palaces be much better than this Corn Palace?'"

"Sounds corny to me," Paul punned. "Thanks for the idea."

"You're welcome," she said. Her mood lightened a little. "I guess we can look on the bright side. Instead of spending the whole day in at the Palace, we only spent an hour. By the looks of things on this road map, we can drive through the Badlands this afternoon and still have time to visit Mount Rushmore tonight."

Paul and Susan both knew why she was in a bad mood over the Corn Palace, and it wasn't because of the Corn Palace. But neither spoke aloud what both thought.

By now the boys had finished their ice cream and fallen asleep in the back seat. The long miles were taking their toll on the family. Everyone was a little worn out. Paul was fighting fatigue at the wheel, so he started talking to Susan about one of the subjects Dr. Vickerson had given him as an assignment.

"You're the English major, so this will be right up your alley," Paul began.

Susan straightened up a little in her seat.

"What are you talking about?" she asked.

"Dr. Vickerson wants me to work on my 'preaching vocabulary.' He gave me a couple of reading assignments to start me in the right direction."

"By 'preaching vocabulary' I hope you don't mean all those technical theology terms you studied in seminary. I'll never forget the time we attended Jon Nelson's ordination service."

"I already know what you're referring to—the preacher who paraded all those huge words before us."

"That's right. Why did Jon ever invite that man to speak?"

"He was Jon's homiletics professor."

"That man? A homiletics professor? No wonder there's a crisis in the pulpits! Remember how badly our pew shook from the youth group losing control? What did Jimmy Morton whisper to you?"

"He said, 'Where'd this guy come from? Does he think he's Roget's Thesaurus?'" Paul laughed. "Then they all started calling him *Thesaurusaurus*! Steve, Lenny, and Doug started giggling so much that they slid down behind the pew in front of them so the speaker couldn't see them.

"*Thesaurusaurus!*" Paul smiled as he reminisced. "Larry commented after the service, 'If he keeps on speaking like this he'll be as extinct as the rest of the dinosaurs before long!'"

"All I remember is biting my hand so hard I almost drew blood to keep from laughing out loud." Susan looked at her hand, half-expecting to see teeth impressions still there 12 years later.

"His sermon theme was 'the eschatological significance of the Parousia as it relates to sundry interpretations of the millennial problem broached by the writer of the Apocalypse in chapter 20,'" Paul intoned deeply and pompously.

"That's it!" Susan howled. In the back seat John moaned and shifted positions and went back to sleep.

"How can you remember after all these years?" she whispered. "And I like your impression, too!"

"I was so proud of myself because I was a middler in seminary, and I knew what all those words meant!" Paul laughed.

"You were probably the only one. I hope this isn't the kind of thing you mean by 'preaching vocabulary.' That kind of language only succeeds in enshrouding the sermon in a theological fog."

"'Enshrouding the sermon in a theological fog!'" Paul repeated. "I like that! That's pretty good for someone who's having trouble staying awake. The sad thing about the message that night was that the man actually had some important things to say, but no one could understand his ridiculous vocabulary.

"What I read was exactly opposite to all this," Paul continued. "I read that the average church member has a working vocabulary of about 7500 words, while the average preacher has a vocabulary of 12,000 words."

"Bet that makes you feel smart."

"Very funny. But of that 7500 words, a third are technical terms dealing specifically with the churchgoer's occupation.

That leaves about 5000 words that the congregation shares in common. Does that sound right to you?"

"It wouldn't surprise me. Americans rank last in the English-speaking world in spelling and use of the language. So what's the point?"

"The point is to keep pulpit language within the limits of the congregation's vocabulary. If I use a technical term I need to clearly define it."

"Even if you take time to define terms they still might sound too complicated, so don't try it too often. Besides, I don't remember Jesus using long, impressive words. He spoke in simple, picturesque language so the common people could understand Him."

"That's precisely the point: I need to work on a vocabulary that uses common language, but in a descriptive way—words that appeal to the five senses—sight, touch, smell, taste, and hearing. That way people will sense what I'm saying, understand it better, and remember it longer."

"So what's your plan?" Susan asked, glancing at the scenery. "I'll be glad when we start seeing some hills again. I'm getting tired of flat flatland. I appreciate the food source of the Great Plains, but what a boring drive! Maybe I should make an observation in your illustration book: 'Contrasts are important in life. If every day were the same—flat, and even-keeled—life would be too dull. We need valleys and mountains, not just the Great Plains!' "

"Very good; write that down. But we also need the Great Plains in our lives to help keep us stable. Imagine if it were all up one hill and down another. The Lord graciously protects us from too much contrast. He gives us no more than we can bear."

"I hope so," sighed Susan.

Both sat quietly for a few miles under the grip of the painful thoughts of things back home.

"Well," Paul said, breaking the long silence, "the way I plan to start strengthening my preaching vocabulary is to become more observant. I'll look for the five senses in what

I encounter, and work at becoming more descriptive, creating word pictures in people's minds.

"When I study various commentaries I'll watch for fresh and expressive vocabulary. For that matter, I'll be on the lookout for it in all my reading."

"Not plagiarism?" Susan asked.

"No, just individual words and short phrases that stand out as especially descriptive. Naturally, if I quote someone more fully I'll give credit where credit is due."

"Don't use too many quotes," she cautioned. "That's just as stuffy as big words."

"I know. I won't."

"Maybe you should buy a pocket dictionary and go through it to circle all the good descriptive terms. That might help."

"That's a great idea! I'll pick one up in Rapid City tonight."

"Paul! We're not stopping in Rapid City to shop for a pocket dictionary! We want to set up camp in time to see Mount Rushmore."

"I know, I know. I'll wait till we're back home. But I like your idea. It's not how large a vocabulary I have, but how well I use language common to the people."

"I think Jon's homiletics professor was more hung up on how brilliant he sounded than on how clearly he communicated. But this makes much more sense. In fact, I can think of the perfect way to summarize all you've told me in just five words," Susan said.

She stopped and waited with a smug smile on her face.

"Just five words? Hurry up. I want to hear this!"

"*Sense appeal, not snob appeal.*"

"Sense appeal, not snob appeal! I like that! Can you write that down for me?"

"I'll be glad to, as long as you give credit where credit is due when you quote me. And since I'm the English major, I'll even throw in an extra quote while I'm at it."

"What's that?"

"One of my college professors loved to quote Pascal, who spoke of 'the eloquence that despises eloquence,'" she responded. "That's what you really want in pulpit language—a way of speaking that is clear, fresh, and powerful, yet without drawing attention to itself. You want the congregation to focus on the message, not the messenger."

"I like that," Paul nodded. "'The eloquence that despises eloquence.' People despise the wrong kind of eloquence. It sounds so highbrow that it builds barriers to communication instead of knocking them down."

"Now that I've given you those two great quotes, I've reached my quot-a, to use one of your silly puns. Wake me up when you see the Golden Arches, please."

With that she propped her pillow against the car door and made herself comfortable. Paul continued thinking over their conversation and how he could use sense appeal and not snob appeal in his pulpit speech. How could he attain that elusive 'eloquence that despises eloquence'? "After all," he thought, "isn't that the eloquence of the Bible itself? Simple, clear, picturesque and powerful language—language that has stood the test of the ages."

Words that appeal to the five senses—sight, touch, smell, taste, and hearing will help people sense what you're saying, understand it better, and remember it longer.

23

Light from Fog

The Badlands provided a great time for the Andrews. New vistas of the strange and wonderful scenery came into view around each bend as the station wagon wound its way back and forth over the serpentine road through the national park.

Paul made several stops so James and John could take quick runs up and down the eerie hillsides. The whole park created a feeling of enchantment due to its strange formations sculpted by the erosion of the soil. While the two boys burned off energies that were stored up from their long ride in the car, Susan and Paul took short excursions on the paths leading out from the turnoff areas.

"Look how much fun they're having," Susan observed as the two boys shouted and waved from the top of a high mound.

"That's why it's so important for us to have this time together, to keep from worrying about matters back at the church," Paul offered as he kicked a small stone out of the path.

"Be careful, boys!" she shouted and waved back. "I agree, Paul. You know, I've been thinking about the situation."

"Yes?'

"Well, I can't imagine the Church Board doing anything bad while we're away. I think they were just so excited to have Dr. Mackey come that they didn't think you'd mind."

"And all those speakers I lined up? Arlene had to call them all on Monday to cancel their preaching."

"I know, but I really don't think Tom meant any harm by it."

"You haven't sat in on some of our Board meetings," Paul grumbled.

"I just have a feeling that things aren't as bad as you imagine. Your preaching has really improved lately. The people have noticed the difference, too."

"You don't think it's a case of too little too late?" Paul asked.

"I don't think so; at least I hope it's not so."

"I hope not, too," replied Paul. "Well, we better head back to the car. It's a long ride to Rushmore."

As Paul and the boys put up the tent at their campsite outside Rapid City, Susan heated a pot of homemade beef stew over the campstove.

"Umm! What smells so good?" asked Paul as he stopped to sniff the air.

"Yeah, mom, what's for dinner?" cried the boys. "We're hungry!"

"Now you appreciate your wife staying up all night to prepare this homemade beef stew for the trip," Susan said. "I know you were annoyed at the time, but I also knew you would enjoy some good home cooking after three days of hamburgers and fast foods."

"You're right about that. Well, boys, let's eat. We need to keep the time in mind. We'll be heading up Mount Rushmore right after supper. I've waited to see that monument for years, and I don't want to miss it now."

The meal was just perfect for James and John, after their earlier climbs in the Badlands. The Andrews finished eating, then cleaned up quickly so they wouldn't be late for the lighting of the monument.

"Dad?" James asked after they had started out in the car.

"Yes, James?"

"What presidents are carved in these rocks?"

"Washington, Jefferson, Lincoln, and . . ." Paul paused, ". . . and I think the fourth is Teddy Roosevelt. He was pretty famous out here. Remember how we read that the Badlands was his favorite place to go."

"My favorite place, too!" said John, thinking of their afternoon fun.

"Mine, too!" added James.

"Well, just wait till we see those faces lit up Mount Rushmore tonight. It will really be neat!" Paul responded.

"I don't know about this, Paul." Susan's voice betrayed anxiety. "It looks like a heavy fog is starting to blanket those mountains."

The Andrews pulled into the parking lot. Dozens of cars in front and behind them had come from all over the country for the same event: the lighting of the monument. The boys counted 14 different state license plates on the cars parked around them.

"We better hurry," Paul urged. "They'll be turning on the lights in a few minutes, and I want good seats."

Paul grabbed James by the hand and Susan took John's. The foursome walked briskly past the slower tourists along the path.

As they reached the outdoor amphitheater, patriotic music was bellowing out over the loudspeakers. Across the chasm in front of them was the side of the mountain bearing the presidents' likenesses. And just above their heads was the fog, rapidly rolling in.

"Come on!" Paul said impatiently as he eyed the fog. "Turn on the lights!"

"The park ranger told me the lights wouldn't go on for another 15 minutes. It needs to be a little darker first," Susan said.

They watched in frustration while the fog kept up its relentless pursuit of the monument. At last the loudspeakers crackled and a voice announced that the lighting ceremony was about to begin. There was a drum roll and the crowd grew quiet in anticipation. Then came the lights, and everybody moaned.

"Fog!" That's all we can see! Fog! I drove 1500 miles from home and all the way up this mountain to see lighted fog!"

"Dad, I don't see any presidents," said James. "Where are their faces?"

"Oh, they're up there, all right," replied their father. "Somewhere behind the fog, they're there."

They sat and watched the lights play on the mist for a few moments, hoping it might clear long enough for a glimpse of the presidents. But to no avail. Little by little the disappointed crowd dispersed and returned to their cars, creating a huge traffic jam on the mountainside. In the background, the pretaped patriotic speech blared on, as if to mock the occasion.

"Not only did the fog ruin our view of the monument, but it also blocks my view of the highway," Paul complained on the way back toward their campsite. "These stupid headlights shine so high into the air that all they light up is the fog. I can't see the road at all."

Suddenly he had an idea. "John, hand me your flashlight. I saw you playing with it in the car on the way up here."

"Sure, dad. What are you going to do with it?"

"Maybe I can shine it on the road until we get down to a lower elevation, out of this foggy soup."

He turned his headlights off and switched on the four-way flashers. Then he rolled down his window and stuck the flashlight out, shining its beam toward the white line marking the shoulder of the highway. Shifting the car into second gear, he proceeded to creep down the mountainside with traffic backed up for miles behind him.

Back at the campsite Paul took out his notebook and began writing about their experience on Mount Rushmore. The boys had fallen asleep on the way down to camp, but he wanted to make his notes before getting them to bed. Susan had also drifted off after they finally got down below the fog level.

"Oh, great. What great illustration have you gotten out of this disaster?" Susan muttered sarcastically. Paul's turning of notebook pages awakened her. With the disappointing events of the day, his rapid scribbling only added to her irritation.

"Oh, a pretty good one," Paul answered, trying not to sound too enthusiastic about it. "We walk by faith and not by sight. Even though the fog covered the faces of those presidents tonight, we know they're still there, carved in the rock. Thousands of tourists climbed that mountain to see them. And tomorrow thousands more will try again. Why? Because we know that they are there. And even though James and John have never seen those faces, they trust their father that those presidents are up there. The same with our God. We know He's there even when our lives are enshrouded with fog. We trust Him in the dark."

"Paul, we haven't even seen those faces, yet alone James and John. I wonder if they're up there myself. And I really don't care to hear any more about it. We drove all this way to see Mount Rushmore by sight, not by faith. Let's get to bed. I've had enough for one day."

"Give me a couple minutes to finish writing."

Susan moaned quietly, "Wake me up when you're done."

As he wrote he glanced back over the previous entries on preaching language she had written just above his remarks on Mount Rushmore. Paul recalled her earlier words about the fog that enshrouded the pulpit.

"That kind of fog is far worse than the fog we experienced tonight!" he thought to himself as he wrote. "Some poor congregations have to grope through foggy preaching week after week. They have no idea where the sermon began, what road it's taking, or what its final destination will be. They can only hope that the face of Christ is hidden somewhere behind all that fog.

"If they survive at all, it's only through their private Bible study and devotional life, sort of the way I had to use John's flashlight to see the road, since my headlights were aimed at the fog.

"Wow!" Paul exclaimed to himself. "This also fits in with that article Dr. Vickerson had me read on the place of applications in the sermon. It said we should put our applications *first* in the sermon instead of the end of the message. When the people know at the beginning that a message will help them overcome their fears or teach them important insights into how they can better cope with life, they'll listen more closely.

"Sometimes preachers work carefully through the exegesis of a passage with the congregation, making them wait until the very end to find out how it all applies to their lives. We should give enough exegesis to help them understand the passage, but most of our work should be left in the study! By hinting where the sermon is going from the beginning, preachers can lift the fog from their congregations' eyes and give them good reason to listen carefully.

"Dr. Vickerson also told me that this was the one place you should use a 'shotgun' rather than a 'rifle.'"

"Wonderful," yawned Susan. "Shoot the congregation."

"No, the shotgun sprays buckshot everywhere, while the rifle fires a single bullet at the target. When you open up the sermon you should fire a round of buckshot so everyone in the congregation knows the message has something in it for them.

"For example, if I were to preach on fear I might begin by listing a couple of dozen different kinds of fears people have: fear of failing, fear of falling, fear of flying, fear of heights, fear of—"

"Fear of losing your job," Susan interrupted.

"Very funny. Yes, fear of losing your job," Paul snapped. "But by shooting off the shotgun you gain the attention of all the different kinds of people in the congregation. If I only spoke about the fear of heights, then anyone who wasn't afraid of heights might tune out the message because they thought it didn't apply to them."

"Are you finished yet?" Susan asked wearily.

"I'm finished," he said, laying down his pen and note-pad.

When the people know at the beginning that a message will help them overcome their fears or teach them important insights into how they can better cope with life, they'll listen more closely.

"We better get the boys into bed. Tomorrow's another long day of travel. I only hope Glacier Park isn't as disappointing as Mount Rushmore."

She turned to awaken the boys, but they were dead to the world.

"I'll get them," Paul offered. "They're getting to be pretty big lizards, but I think I can still manage them."

He opened the back door, gently picked up James, and carried him into the tent. Susan had gone ahead and opened the sleeping bag for him. Then as she opened John's bag and prepared it, Paul returned to the car. He could tell by John's breathing that he was playing the fox, but he made no comment. Something felt so good about having dad carry him to bed like this, and he didn't want to spoil that for John, especially since James already had his turn.

After the two boys were bedded down, Paul and Susan crawled under the covers, exhausted from the long day. It was a day that began at the Corn Palace, wound its way through the Badlands, and ended up dying on the foggy mountaintop.

"Honey," Paul whispered.

"Huh?"

"Are you asleep yet?"

"Almost. Why?"

"I just wanted to ask you one question."

"If it's about preaching I think I'll strangle you."

"No, it's not about preaching."

"Come on, I want to get to sleep," Susan grumbled. "What's your question?"

Paul was barely able to contain himself. Finally, after gaining enough control, he blurted it out:

"Are we having fun yet?"

The next thing he felt was a swift pillow to the face.

24

Campfire Reflections on Preaching

One evening en route to Glacier National Park Paul helped James and John build the campfire they had been so anxious to have. After their supper they paused to have their family devotions as they huddled together around the warm fire. Paul read from the first Psalm and led a little discussion with Susan and the boys on the importance of listening to the advice and counsel of godly rather than wicked people.

After the devotional time Susan pointed out that much of the power of the Psalm was found in its descriptive use of imagery.

"What makes Psalm 1 so vivid and easy to remember are its great word pictures: the tree planted by the waters contrasted to the chaff blown away by the wind," she said enthusiastically.

"These are similes because they use the words 'like' or 'as' to set up the comparison. But if they had dropped those words, they would become metaphors: 'The godly are trees planted by rivers of waters.'

Paul studied her warm and cheerful face by the light of the crackling campfire. It was terrible how the busyness of life back home crowded in on these special moments together. Vacation served to rekindle that relationship. He was so grateful that they had been able to trust the Lord enough to go on with their trip and try to put church problems aside during this time.

"Paul, are you listening?" she asked, aware by the look on his face that he might be somewhere else.

"Sure I am. You're giving me an English lecture."

"No, I'm giving you a preaching lecture! Now listen to the difference between these two statements," she continued. "I am the vine and you are the branches."

"That's from John 15," Paul noted.

Meanwhile James and John had managed to find the bag with the Hershey's chocolate bars and graham crackers, and they were toasting marshmallows over the fire in order to make s'mores.

"I know it's from John 15, but listen to the difference."

"Did you really know?" Paul challenged teasingly. "If I had asked you where that was from, would you have been able to say 'John 15'?"

"Will you be quiet and listen to me, Paul Andrews!"

"Aha! See, you don't know, do you?"

"In another minute I'm going to put you on a stick and roast you over the campfire!"

James and John looked up. Susan's last remark caught their attention, and their eyes grew big in anticipation of what might happen next. They knew it was all in fun, but they always liked to watch where the fun would lead them. To their disappointment, Paul allowed Susan to continue her little speech.

"If I turn Jesus' metaphor into a simile, listen to how it sounds: I am *like* a vine, and you are *like* its branches."

"Doesn't quite have the punch!" Paul laughed.

"Right—the simile weakens the tension in the analogy; the metaphor has more power. Because of the imagery of those kinds of comparisons, people remember them for a long time. And by remembering the images they connect them back to the point of the analogy.

"For example, you once asked the question: What is a body, a bride, a building, and a battalion, all in one?"

"You actually remember that sermon?"

"Those are all metaphors for the church. Do you see the power in the metaphor? Aristotle said that 'the greatest thing by far was to be master of the metaphor.'"

"Now you're quoting Aristotle! Am I impressed!"

"The only thing you're going to be impressed with is this stick!" she feigned anger while holding up John's marshmallow stick.

"Speaking of sticks, let me have it," said Paul. "I'm getting hungry for one of those s'mores."

"Oh, I'll let you have it all right." She gently poked at him, then handed over the stick and returned to her lecture.

"Jesus called His followers the "light of the world" and the "salt of the earth," and no one has ever forgotten it since. He was also fond of similes. Remember how often He said, 'The kingdom of heaven is like...'?"

"'Like a mustard seed,' for one," Paul responded. "Yes, I see what you mean. I can think of 'whitewashed sepulchers,' and back in the Old Testament Ephraim was 'a cake not turned'—in other words, half-baked. You're right—those images are easy to remember."

"And they keep people thinking about the comparison. So try to use more metaphors and similes in your sermon. Whenever you want to get a point across in a powerful, memorable way, try to think of a good analogy or figure of speech to describe it."

"By the way," asked Paul, "why do you know so much about all the metaphors and similes in the Bible?"

"I went to a Christian college, remember? Our English professor loved to give us our assignments from the various writing methods used in the Bible."

By the time they reached Glacier National Park, Paul was thoroughly relaxed. Glacier's breathtaking beauty helped take his mind off church work. Tom Fedderhoffer, Larry Lyons, and the church draperies were as distant as the separation in miles. He managed to scribble off a post-card to Dr. Vickerson, but he never thought of Dr. Vickerson's friendship in the same light as church problems.

There was the ten-mile hike up to Iceberg Lake and back, complete with bells the boys had to wear to warn the grizzly bears they were on the trail. There were the shaggy white mountain goats with their comical faces and beards. They were so tame that James and John would have walked right up to pet them had their worried mother not intervened.

Occasionally Susan had to remind Paul to write down illustrations of what they saw. One in particular was a touching memorial at the visitors' center at the summit of Logan's Pass. Susan discovered a plaque in memory of a young man who had died in a fall while mountain-climbing. She cried as she read:

> In loving memory of Dr. Charles Bauer, who
> met his Savior Jesus on his favorite mountain,
> Mt. Reynolds, in Glacier National Park.

"He died on May 31, 1986. He was only 29 years old."

"What a witness to the Lord," Paul replied soberly. "And of all places, here in a national park visitor center."

"Just look at the love of Christ in this man's eyes, Paul." She pointed to his picture next to the memorial plaque. Below it were his climbing gear, rope, and other equipment.

What really astounded them was how none of the employees they questioned at the visitors' center even knew that the display was there.

"I'll be sure to use this in a sermon when we get home," Paul said. "Here's a great witness of Christ to the world, and the world seems to pass on by." He wrote the exact quote from the plaque on the back of one of the park brochures. Later he transferred it to his notepad.

Their last day at Glacier led to a discussion on the place of humor in the sermon. A young seminarian preached at the national park Sunday worship service. His message was filled with jokes and one-liners from beginning to end.

"He sounded more like a stand-up comic than a preacher," Susan complained.

"I don't mind jokes, but there wasn't much substance in the message," Paul added. "It sure was nice to sit with my family, though."

"It felt good to have you with us," Susan agreed. "People would be surprised to know that the thing I hate most about the ministry is what it has done to our weekends. You tense up on Saturday nights, and even though you may be home with us, you're not really with us. Remember back when we were first married? Sunday was my favorite day of the week!"

"Mine, too," said Paul. It was so relaxing to go to church and sit together, to spend the whole day with each other. Now we only get to do this four weeks out of the year."

"I liked that joke about the mosquito that bit the preacher and flew away singing, 'There's Power in the Blood!'" giggled James.

"I didn't!" frowned Susan "I thought it was sacrilegious."

"What's 'sack religion'?" asked John.

"It's the most popular religion in America," Paul laughed. "While people wake up to go to church on Sunday mornings, millions more stay in the sack. They attend St. Mattress."

"Huh?" John said with a blank face.

"Be serious, Paul," Susan said, trying hard to keep a straight face. "Honey, the word is 'sacrilegious.' It refers to when people make light of or make fun of the holy things of God."

"When your mother said his joke was sacrilegious," Paul added, "she meant we should never joke about the blood of Christ. He paid so dearly for our salvation that it just isn't right to joke about it."

"I like humor that's more natural," commented Susan. "I like it when someone sees humor in the situations of life rather than telling corny jokes and puns."

"Maybe, but we think Jesus used puns," Paul countered. "The Aramaic for camel is *gamla* and for gnat is *galma*. Or is it the other way around? Anyway, He told the Pharisees they strain out the *galma* and swallow the *gamla*!"

"I didn't know you studied Aramaic."

"I didn't, but you know me and puns."

"Do I ever!" groaned his wife. "But I prefer the humor of exaggeration and hyperbole. Take the example you just mentioned. Can you imagine the Pharisees straining out gnats and swallowing camels?"

"Humps and all?" cried James.

"Humps and all," laughed Susan.

"I don't get it. How could anyone swallow a whole camel?" James replied.

"That's just the point. You can't . . . oh, forget it, James." Susan shook her head in frustration, then added, "You'll understand someday."

"So you like the kind of humor that kids don't get!" laughed Paul.

"Very funny. It's more natural because you can tailor it to fit your sermon's purpose. The jokes preachers tell rarely relate to the message. They do more harm than good because they send the congregation off on a tangent."

"But humor is helpful. It eases tensions, and makes the time go faster. It keeps the congregation alert and listening. I think it's important," Paul countered.

"But it should strengthen the message, not weaken it. How often have people gone home on Sunday and thought,

'Now what was that joke the preacher told? Wait till I tell the guys at work!' They never connect the joke to the message, so the whole point is missed!"

"That young seminarian's jokes weren't even vaguely related to his message."

"So how is God glorified in that?"

Susan looked at her husband, who suddenly grew distant.

"Paul, what is it?"

"Oh, nothing," he shrugged. "I was thinking how we're sitting here in Glacier criticizing that poor seminarian, and I wonder what comparisons have been going on back at Calvary Church. Dr. Mackey's preaching is so powerful. What do the people say about my preaching when I'm not around?"

"Paul, don't worry about it. The way you've been preaching these last couple of months, I'm sure they're saying good things about you," she assured.

"Yeah, I suppose." Paul remained unconvinced, despite Susan's efforts to build his confidence.

The following morning the Andrews got an early start for Mount Rainier in Washington State.

At Rainier, Paradise was just as Dr. Vickerson described it—*almost* Paradise.

"I imagine it isn't so wonderful up here when these beautiful meadow flowers are buried in 20 feet of snow," Paul commented while reading about the annual snowfall in a park brochure. "No place on earth is quite Paradise."

"Only heaven is heaven," Susan added. "But this sure is a taste of it. The Lord is so good, Paul. How fortunate you are to have a job that allows you a whole month away with your family!"

"Mom! Dad!" the boys shouted as they rushed up in excitement. "When can we play in the snow?"

"Who said you could play in the snow?" asked Susan.

"That boy over there!" shouted John. He pointed to a young boy playing beside a camper across the road from them.

"He said you don't even need coats and gloves, it's so warm up where the snow is!" added James breathlessly. "Can we go right now? Can we?" begged the boys.

"We'll go after breakfast," said Susan. "Can you imagine that, Paul? Snow in the middle of summer!"

"I guess if there will be snow in the real Paradise, it would have to be in the summer there, too," quipped Paul.

When the time came to leave Mount Rainier, Paul and Susan were struck with the same thought. The sights of Glacier and Rainier were so breathtaking and satisfying that they felt no need to go any further west. They decided to start for home.

"We've been sleeping in this tent for over two weeks now, and I'm starting to miss the old bed back home," said Paul.

"I am too," agreed Susan. "Besides, we ought to leave some more for us to see if we ever make it back to the Northwest again!"

25

The Tale of the Tapes

"Are we ready to order now?" asked the young waitress.

"I didn't know you were joining us for dinner," Paul replied.

"Please forgive my husband," Susan blushed as she elbowed him. "His sense of humor is a little strange at times."

"But she asked, 'Are *we* ready to order yet?'" Paul persisted.

"Just ignore him!" Susan exclaimed.

The waitress' blank face showed she had no idea what he meant. The hungry family placed its orders for Sunday dinner, then waited impatiently for the food to come.

"I hate it when you do that!" Susan snapped at Paul after the waitress left the table. "People never know how to take that kind of humor!"

"But she said, 'Are *we* ready to order yet?' Paul quoted. "Why do all waitresses ask that? Why don't they ask, 'Are *you* ready to order yet?'"

"I don't know. Probably for the same reason you preachers always say *we* instead of *you*."

"What do you mean by that?" he asked defensively.

"Like the time you were preaching on Zaccheus' great repentance as a sinful tax collector. You told the congregation, and I quote, 'We must confess our sins when we cheat on our taxes like Zaccheus did.' The way you said it sounded like *you* had been cheating on *your* taxes."

"Were you cheating, dad?" John looked up in stunned unbelief.

"No, he wasn't," assured his mother. "But the way he said it, he sounded as if he had."

"What are you suggesting I should have said?"

"Maybe you should try speaking in the second person for a change. Say 'you must repent' rather than 'we must repent.'"

"Then I'd offend people because it sounds like I'm preaching at them," Paul growled. "That's all I need to do to drive out a few more members!"

"But that's the way Jesus preached. He said, 'Woe to you, Pharisees!'"

"But I'm not Jesus! Jesus was sinless, remember? And I'm a sinner. There's a big difference."

"John the Baptist was a sinner, yet he spoke that way. Even though he was unworthy to untie Jesus' shoes, he confronted sinners—and he got beheaded for his boldness!"

"Are you suggesting my preaching isn't bold enough? Or that you'd like to see me beheaded?" Paul's anger and hurt were growing with each exchange.

"No, I'm not, Honey," she soothed. "But using the second person properly would make more sense at times, and I think it conveys more power. I think *we* weakens the message. It makes preachers sound like they must first shoot themselves before they're permitted to shoot the congregation."

"Who wants to shoot the congregation? I'm trying to share God's Word with them," Paul fired back.

As soon as the words came out he recalled his conversation with Dr. Vickerson about the difference between rifles and shotguns and how his message should be aimed for the hearer's heart with all the precision of a sharpshooting rifleman.

The message should have a clear purpose, a target. Like the rifle, it should be aimed carefully at that target to hit the mark.

"Well, maybe I am, in a way," he mumbled after a long pause.

She stared blankly at him, but before she could pursue that odd admission, the waitress returned with their food.

"Do you care to join us?" Paul teased the waitress.

"Thank you, but I have others to wait on," she answered courteously. Then as she walked away, in fear she might have offended him, she turned and said, "Maybe next time I won't be too busy with customers to join you folks. Thanks very much for the generous offer."

At that, Susan almost choked on her mouthful of salad.

"Serves you right for eating before we pray!" Paul snapped. His bad mood made him suppress the urge to laugh.

After eating, he cheered up again. He realized that some of his irritability was due to hunger. But he knew the major portion of it was due to his sensitivity over the situation back home. Now that they were heading home again his anxieties over things at Calvary Church had created a small knot in his stomach. But realizing the problem helped him to adjust to it and lighten his spirits once again.

Susan drove the afternoon stretch, while he used the time to read the Sermon on the Mount and portions of sermons in Acts. Susan's intuition about preaching in the second person proved a valuable insight. He was hard-pressed to find any place where the apostles used "we" rather than "you."

He also took out his sermon tapes on Jonah and began to listen critically to his own preaching. As he played back his sermons on a portable cassette player, he used earphones to spare his family the agony of listening to three hours of his preaching. He kept his notepad beside him, and occasionally stopped the tape to write observations on areas for improvement.

He listened closely for his use of "we" instead of "you." He wrote down key statements from his tapes, then stopped the tape long enough to reword them in the second person. By simply changing "we" to "you" his messages gained a sense of urgency and power.

Other key areas involved introductions and conclusions, since they also lacked power and purpose. He often fumbled through the opening of his sermons with annoying "ers" and "ahs," but after he got on track and gained confidence they disappeared. He remembered again how Dr. Vickerson had said this was one place to fire the shotgun, to start the sermon with an attention-getting bang that fired in enough different directions to grab the ears of the different groups and individuals that made up his audience.

"My sermons begin more with a self-conscious dull thud rather than a confident, powerful blast from the gun!" Paul lamented to himself. "I must prepare my introductions more carefully."

Likewise, he noticed that his sermons often ended more like a whimper than a bang because he failed to bring his messages to proper and fitting conclusions. Usually this reflected back on the need to have that clear purpose statement as his sermon's target and destination. The conclusion was the final effort to drive the message home to the heart of the hearers.

Paul pondered the idea of using a full manuscript to overcome these problems, but he knew how the congregation would react to reading sermons. He also realized how poor his eye contact would be if he resorted to written sermons. He decided to discipline himself to write out the introductions and conclusions, along with key statements that would overcome hesitation in transitions. Although he might take the written statements into the pulpit with him, Paul intended to memorize them well enough so he would not have to read them to the congregation.

He also noted the painful fact that at times his sermons really dragged, and that his voice wasn't nearly as expressive and strong as he thought it sounded. This surprised him, because these things are hard to sense from the pulpit, but easy to notice from the pew.

He made a list of ways to correct this and rid his sermons of boredom. First, he intended to place a large sign on the pulpit with one word written on it: *Enthusiasm!* This would serve to remind him to speak out, to preach with abandon. He also intended to practice on tape to get more acquainted with the volume level of his voice.

His list also included the need for more picturesque language and the need to reword or discard worn-out clichés and phrases that he tended to fall back on from week to week as he preached. Listening to several messages in one sitting helped him to discover tedious patterns. He listed the need to add illustrations and to employ appropriate humor.

He reflected on how frequent commercial breaks on television and radio had conditioned the modern mind to shorter attention spans. He needed to constantly keep the sermon moving, yet without interrupting its continuity, in order to better hold the congregation's interest. "If it's worth saying, it's worth saying in an interesting way," he wrote to himself. "What good is a good insight if the people tune me out before I get to it?"

Somewhere in the middle of his fourth sermon Paul nodded off and began snoring loudly. Susan and the boys laughed long and hard at this preacher sleeping through his own sermons. Their laughter, loud as it was, never roused him. They knew then and there that he would not live that one down as long as he lived.

After supper Paul decided he was ready to drive straight home.

"You're kidding!" said Susan. "We still have almost 500 miles to go!"

"It's either that or put up the tent one more night. Personally, I'd rather drive all night than do that. You can all sleep while I drive, then I'll catch up when I land on that nice, soft bed waiting for me at home."

"Just so you don't land on the side of the road in a ditch somewhere. Aren't you afraid you'll fall asleep at the wheel?"

"Don't worry, I'll be fine. I'm up for doing this."

"Just promise me you won't listen to any more of your sermon tapes!" Susan teased.

"Oh, no, dad, please don't!" shouted the boys. Then both began to imitate their father's loud snoring.

"Very funny. Why do I feel so outnumbered in this car?"

The Andrews talked and laughed all the way until midnight. It felt so warm and cozy all together in their station wagon. But soon the vacation would be over. The busyness of church life back home would try hard to crowd out their precious times as a family.

As Paul drove through the night, his wife fell into a deep sleep beside him. He smiled as he glanced over his shoulder at the boys. They tossed restlessly back and forth. John's head was at one end of the seat, with James' at the other. Their legs were twisted and tangled up in a strange formation.

By starting for home earlier than they had planned, and by his determination to drive through the night, the family would arrive home a whole week early. In the quietness of the early hours he began to plan the little projects he would do around the house with the extra time. He was happy he didn't have to preach for one more Sunday, but thoughts of Dr. Mackey in the pulpit quickly dampened his enthusiasm.

As he drove on in the starry darkness, he wondered what had been happening back at Calvary Church during his absence. He got a sick feeling in his stomach thinking about the unwanted surprises waiting for him after previous vacations. He tried to shrug it off as he thought of the words he read earlier in Matthew 5-7. "Don't worry about tomorrow, Paul," he said to himself. "Just spend time praising God for this great vacation and this wonderful family He has given me. Don't worry about Calvary Church. It can all wait until you get back home."

26

Home at Last!

Paul nudged his wife.

"We're home," he whispered.

Susan slowly opened her eyes.

"Honey, you should see yourself in a mirror right now!" Paul laughed.

She started to stretch slowly, but stopped suddenly and groaned. Her awkward sleeping position over the last few hours left her body complaining.

"You don't look like much of a prize yourself, marathon man," she muttered. "How did you ever do it? Where are we, anyway?"

"We're inside the garage. I shut the door so nobody will realize we're home yet. I'm going up to bed. Don't let anyone wake me up!"

"Look at those two sons of thunder," Susan said, nodding toward the back seat. "Such thunder! Don't you love it when they're sleeping like that? They're so precious."

"If they're so precious, why do you only say so when they're sleeping?" Paul smiled.

Paul opened the car door and stumbled out while Susan awakened the boys. Slowly they untangled themselves and crawled out.

"Did we pick up Snooper yet?" James mumbled.

"No, honey," his mother replied. "We'll worry about Snooper and the goldfish later. Right now let's get some sleep. And if you boys wake up before your dad and I do, please play quietly. Remember, while you were sleeping daddy was up driving all night."

"What time is it?" yawned John.

"It's about 5:30 in the morning. So get up to your bedroom and get a few more hours' sleep."

Paul stopped at the massive pile of mail which the neighbors had faithfully stacked on the kitchen table. They came each day the Andrews were gone, and checked the house, brought in the mail, and watered the plants.

"Anything important?" asked Susan on the way up the stairs.

"Lots of bills and tons of junk mail!"

Paul fell into a deep sleep as soon as his head hit the pillow. Late in the afternoon the sun shone through his bedroom window, making the room unbearably hot. He awoke to find himself and his bedsheets soaked with sweat. As he came to, his whole body began to ache like he had been run over by a truck.

He heard Susan talking quietly on the phone down in the kitchen. She had been up since 9:30, thanks to James and John. So she made the boys unpack the car while she tackled the massive pile of laundry. By the time Paul awakened she had almost everything but the luggage put away. Sleeping bags and blankets were draped over the clothesline out back, and the clothes were already dry and folded in the blue laundry basket.

She began to laugh when she saw Paul stumble into the kitchen. His hair was sticking out in every direction, and the bedding had left red wrinkle lines in strange patterns all over the side of his face.

"Mom, you should see your son!" she said to the caller on the other end. "He just woke up. I really don't think you would recognize him."

"Tell mom I said 'hi,'" he mumbled. "I can't believe you got all this work done. If it weren't so hot up in that bedroom, I could have slept all night."

"She says 'hi' and 'I love you,'" Susan said, covering the mouthpiece as she relayed the message.

"Mom, I'll talk to you later. I better take care of your baby. Yes, we love you too. We'll be over to pick up Snooper sometime tomorrow. Okay? Bye now."

After Susan filled Paul in on all the latest family gossip, he went back upstairs and took a long, cool bath in the tub. Later they drove to the supermarket to stock their empty refrigerator and stopped on the way back at their favorite ice cream stand.

The following morning Paul drove to the church office, where his secretary, Arlene, happily greeted him.

"Paul, you're back early! How was your trip?"

"I'll tell you all about it, but first let me have all the bad news," Paul said with a nervous laugh. "Who died while I was gone? Who's getting ready to leave the church? Hit me with all the gory details!"

"Such a pessimist for a man of God!" Arlene laughed. "You'd be surprised how well we got along without you."

"That's what scares me most," he replied.

"Everyone's healthy and fine. Even Larry Lyons has been back in church for two weeks now."

"Larry!" Paul exclaimed.

"Yes, Larry. He looks a little pale yet from his open heart surgery, but he seems to be coming along fine. Why the frown, Paul?"

"I just remembered—Larry's a big fan of Dr. Mackey's. He'll probably stop coming again after I get back to the pulpit."

"I don't think so, not the way he's talking. I think surgery helped him realize how important this congregation is to him."

"I hope you're right," Paul said doubtfully. "He and Tom Fedderhoffer must be in their glory with Dr. Mackey here and me on vacation."

"Watch it, Paul," she cautioned. "Tom's somewhere in the building right now. A couple of pews came loose from the kids rocking them during church, and you know Tom. He says he'll bolt 'em to the floor if he has to."

Paul laughed. "Did he mean the kids or the pews?"

"I hope he meant the pews."

"Well, I'd better say hello to him. I'll be back in a few moments."

Paul found Tom right where Arlene suggested he would be—flat on his stomach underneath the back pew, holding an electric drill in his big fist. Sweat was pouring down his face and neck, and his shirt was wet. All the sanctuary windows were tightly shut, trapping the hot, musty air inside.

"What are you doing under there with that drill?" Paul called out. "Trying to make this place a little holier?"

"A pun like that can only come from one person," Tom said as he crawled out from under the pew. "It's good to see you, Paul! You're back early, aren't you?"

He reached out and shook Paul's hand warmly. Paul was surprised at the intensity of his enthusiastic greeting.

"How was your vacation? Everything go all right?"

"Tremendous. We had a wonderful time. We came back a couple of days early, and my curiosity got the best of me. I had to see how things were at the church. By the way, how's Dr. Mackey?"

"He's fine. Wilma and I had Mac and Ev over for dinner

after church last Sunday. What a man of God! His coming here means so much to me."

As Tom spoke of Dr. Mackey, Paul observed the glow of admiration in his eyes. He tried to keep it from bothering him, but in the few minutes since they began the conversation, all the old hurts had returned.

"Paul, I never told you how I first met Dr. Mackey."

"No, I don't think you have," Paul said as he managed to smile politely.

"I was a young man," Tom began as he put down his drill. "I had just returned from the Korean War. I had been strong in the heat of the battle. While others around me were cracking up from the strain, I always kept my cool. Then when I got home I fell apart. I became very confused. Frankly, I was lost!

"One night some old high school friends came over and suggested we go to an evangelistic meeting at a church nearby. They thought we'd all get a big kick out of watching some kind of holy stage show. It was the last thing in the world I wanted to do, but I finally gave in."

Paul listened with deepening interest. In all his ten years at Calvary he had never seen this side of Tom Fedderhoffer.

Tom's eyes welled up as he continued. "Turned out to be the turning point in my life. Of course, the speaker that night was Dr. Mackey. At the time he was still Pastor Mackey, and he asked everyone to call him Mac.

"Well, I sat and I squirmed, and I began to think he prepared that message just for me. For a moment I got angry about it. I figured maybe somebody had tipped him off about me. How else could he know so much about my heart?

"Then I realized how foolish that was. God was speaking to me that night, not Pastor Mackey. The rest of the guys kept laughing and giggling in the back of the church, but the more he talked, the more I listened. Finally they got up to leave in the middle of his sermon, but I refused to go with them. Those guys made fun of me every time they saw me after that. I knew they would, but I didn't care. I never thought I needed God before, but that night I realized what a weak and helpless sinner I was without Christ.

"At the end of his message, Mac invited anyone who wanted to trust Christ to come up front and meet with him to pray. I hadn't been to church since I was a child in Sunday school, and I had no idea what was going to happen, but that night I almost ran to the front.

"I was a little surprised to see that I was the only one who came up, but I really didn't care. I knew God was calling me, and that's all that counted.

"My life has never been the same since. I began to attend that little church every week. I started to read my Bible and pray. Then one Sunday I met Wilma after the service, and we started dating. When our wedding day came, Dr. Mackey was the one who married us. Later, when the kids came along, it was Dr. Mackey who baptized them. I'm so indebted to that man, Paul. You'll never know how much!"

Tears were now streaming down Tom's cheeks. It seemed strange to see this tough ex-Marine crying. Deep inside himself, Paul felt like he had just been hit with a sledgehammer.

"That's a wonderful story, Tom. Why didn't you ever tell me this before?"

"When you came here you were just a kid out of seminary, Paul. I'm still a Marine at heart. You know, once a Marine, always a Marine. You had never been in the military, and you were so young and inexperienced. I guess I didn't feel right talking to you about it. I'm sorry I waited so long."

"That's okay, it means even more to me that you waited till now. Dr. Mackey's quite a preacher! I heard him in chapel when I was in seminary. He made a big impression on all the students."

"Since you're home early, you'll get to hear him again this Sunday."

"I'm afraid not. Susan and I have other plans."

"That's too bad, but I'd still like you to meet him sometime."

"I'd like that."

"Paul, I want you to know something. Dr. Mackey isn't the preacher he once was. A lot of the stories he's told us this month I've heard him use before. It made me appreciate how hard your job is. You have to preach week after week to the same people. Someone like Mac can take his best sermons and his best illustrations and use them over and over everywhere he goes. But you have to come up with something new and fresh to say each time.

"I'm not trying to be critical of Dr. Mackey, but his use of witnessing encounters from years ago made me wonder if he has been involved in any present witnessing opportunities. To me part of the power of a sermon is to hear that someone is out there on the cutting edge right now. The battles are being fought *today* for Christ, and there are soldiers in the trenches waging war for Him. Dr. Mackey preached the same sermons I heard him preach years ago. Back then those sermons were fresh and powerful, but today they were as stale as yesterday's news."

"But the gospel is always the power of God unto salvation. It never gets old," Paul countered gently.

"I know, and I believe that. But that's the very reason why the illustrations of how that gospel is reaching the world should come from today's battlefronts, not yesterday's."

"I know what you mean. There's a special thrill to hear that someone just yesterday or last week has been conquered by the power of Christ."

"That's exactly what I mean."

Tom paused, then looked directly at Paul. "I couldn't tell you this before, but I can now. Your preaching has really improved the last few months. I've sensed that you've been entering the pulpit each week having had a fresh encounter with Christ and having returned from the battlefield to give us a progress report.

"Somebody's lit a fire under you, Paul," the former Marine continued. "I don't know who or what or how, but whatever it is, keep up the good work. I know I haven't been in your corner very often; I apologize for that, and I promise things will be different from now on."

Paul stood in stunned silence. Usually he had to smile a little at Tom's warfare terminology. But today he was speechless. Finally he sputtered out a thank you.

Tom reached out and shook Paul's hand again. It was with his usual firmness that he gripped Paul's hand, but the enthusiasm with which he shook it was wholehearted and genuine.

"I'd better get back to these pews. Wilma's expecting me soon. See you next Sunday."

"Just one more thing, Tom," Paul said, seeing a golden opportunity to put his "Nehemiah Project" into action.

"Sure, what's that?"

"One difference in me has been my determination to make preaching a top priority in my minstry. I've done a little time study on my work here at Calvary, and I'd like to share the results with the Church Board. That way we can discuss ways I can better use my time. You may have noticed a difference already, but I still have a long way to go. I want to keep improving. It's for the congregation's good as well as my own. But that's going to require some changes in my role here."

"Sounds good to me, Paul. Like I said, I'm in your corner from now on. Whatever I can do to help, let me know."

"Could I have breakfast with you and a couple others on the Board when I get back to work next week? Maybe we can get this new fall season off to a great start."

"Sounds like an excellent idea. Call me first thing next week."

Paul wandered back to the church office in a daze.

"Arlene, you'll never believe the conversation I just had with Tom."

"You mean he told you he actually likes your preaching?" she laughed.

"That, and more."

"I know. He was in here earlier telling me about the big improvement he's seen in your sermons. He said that as much as he loves Dr. Mackey, he's really looking forward to hearing you in the pulpit again!"

"I can't believe this. First, Larry Lyons comes back, then Tom tells me he likes my preaching! I better go home and start the day over again—all that driving has affected my brain."

"It's not the driving, it's all the praying and hard work, Paul. You know a lot of us have been praying very hard for you this past year. We love you and know how tough this time has been on you and Susan."

"Thanks, Arlene. It seems the Lord has been answering those prayers, doesn't it?"

Paul felt himself welling up now, so he quickly abandoned the soberness of the conversation. "Still, I'd better go home to rest and recuperate from the shock. If anyone needs me, tell them I'm in therapy and can't be reached!"

On the way home in the car Paul wept joyfully at the amazing reception he had experienced from Tom. In between his praising the Lord, he reflected on Tom's insights into preaching. What he observed as a weakness in Dr. Mackey's sermons spelled the potential for disaster in the weekly preaching of a pastor. Paul realized all the more how important it was to live his ministry on the cutting edge. Not only should his sermons include recent witnessing encounters with the lost, but they should also reflect his conversations with believers and unbelievers concerning the whole counsel of God.

> *Part of the power of a sermon is to hear that someone is out there on the cutting edge right now. Enter the pulpit each week having had a fresh encounter with Christ and having returned from the battlefield to give a progress report.*

He realized he had to do this without betraying any counseling situations. Perhaps he could poll various people, members and nonmembers alike, on their feelings and beliefs on an upcoming sermon topic. That way he could take the pulse of the congregation and the surrounding community, and then, armed with such insights, he could enter the pulpit more fully prepared to hit the bull's-eye. The polling would not be scientific, but informal.

Paul's excitement with the idea grew. He could even use this as an opportunity for witnessing. His questions might pique the interest of those he would be polling, thereby opening the door to further conversations with them. Paul decided to try out his idea during the next few months and making it part of his preaching seminar—thanks to the insights on preaching from Tom Fedderhoffer!

"Maybe if I listen more closely to the people in the pews, I might gain other insights, too!" Paul thought to himself as he turned onto his street.

He pulled the car into the driveway and raced in to tell Susan the latest news. As she listened, she began to cry.

"Can you believe it, honey?" Paul asked. "After all that worry over the church!"

"Paul, I'm so glad to hear it," Susan cried with joy. "I was beginning to think we'd have to move. This means we can stay at Calvary Church. We can keep our home. Our kids can stay in school with their friends and classmates. Paul, I'm so happy."

"I didn't realize how much this was affecting you," he said. "You've always been so reassuring."

"You were so discouraged. I'm sorry for snapping at you when I did. I really tried not to put any more pressure on you than you already had. And I do believe in the power of prayer. It just surprises me sometimes the way God answers us!" she laughed and cried at the same time.

"I have to call Dr. Vickerson. He'll be glad to hear this too. That man has prayed for me so much!"

Paul's efforts at reaching Dr. Vickerson were unsuccessful.

"I wonder if he's still at his sister's place," he said as he put down the receiver.

He called again later in the day, letting the phone ring several times to allow the professor enough time to reach it. No answer.

The whole family was still reeling a little from the effects of their marathon drive home. After a quick trip to pick up Snooper, they returned and went to bed early. James and John were especially cranky in the car and needed their rest.

Later that evening, the phone startled Susan and Paul from a deep sleep. The red digitals on their alarm clock registered 11:15.

"Now who's so ignorant to call this late?" Paul grumbled as he straightened up in bed. "Maybe we should let it ring. We're still on vacation, you know."

"You better get it. It could be important, Paul." Susan gently nudged him out of bed.

"Okay, okay, I'm coming," he shouted at the phone.

27

The Late Night Phone Call

"Hello?"

"Pastor Andrews?" asked the voice on the other end of the line.

"Yes, this is Pastor Andrews. May I help you?"

"Pastor, I'm so glad I've reached you. I was afraid you wouldn't be home yet. I'm Ethel Bradford, William Vickerson's sister," she said.

"Mrs. Bradford? Oh, yes. Dr. Vickerson has told me a lot about you."

As he spoke, Paul realized something was wrong. He pulled out a chair and slowly sat down at the kitchen table.

"Is Dr. Vickerson okay?" he asked.

"I'm sorry to call with such bad news, Pastor Andrews, but my brother died early this morning."

Paul sank down in his chair. "I can't believe this. What happened?"

By now Susan had come down from the bedroom and sat at the foot of the hallway steps. From there she watched and listened. Paul cupped the phone and whispered, "Dr. Vickerson's dead!"

"My brother was recovering quite well from his surgery. In fact, the doctor told us yesterday..."

"Wait a minute," interrupted Paul. "What surgery? I don't know anything about this."

"I'm sorry. I forgot you didn't know. That must make this doubly shocking."

"Shocking isn't the word," Paul said softly.

"He said he intended to tell you beforehand, but after he found out you were going on vacation he decided his surgery would only cause you needless worry while you were away."

"I can't believe this," said Paul. "He told me you insisted he visit because his close friend had died."

"Well, that's true. His surgery wasn't to take place until Monday of last week, but when I heard how depressed he sounded I encouraged him to come earlier. What he didn't tell you was that back in early July his doctor discovered a tumor on his left lung. When he insisted on surgery, Vic asked him to recommend a specialist in our area so we could take care of him during his recovery.

"He was coming along fine, but then late last night after we left the hospital he went into cardiac arrest. They worked with him for several hours, but he never recovered. We think maybe a clot broke loose and went to the heart. We're just not sure."

"He didn't seem to be suffering much from the tumor— or at least he kept it well hidden," Paul said, "although I did notice how hard his breathing was at times. But I just thought it was due to his arthritis and the extra labor of walking with that cane."

"It came as a total shock to us all," Mrs. Bradford replied. "The doctor told him that many times this kind of cancer doesn't cause much pain until it's in its final stages."

"I can't believe this," Paul kept repeating.

"It's a blessing he died, Pastor Andrews. His cancer had already metastasized, so he would have required radiation and chemotherapy as soon as his body was strong enough for it. We envisioned more surgery and more therapy down the road. The Lord was merciful to take him home."

"He's home," repeated Paul. "Home with his Lord and with Emily. What are the plans for the funeral?"

"That's why I'm so glad we reached you, Pastor. I tried the church office around five this afternoon, but all I got was the answering service. Then I called your number, but you didn't answer."

"We went to pick up our dog. That's probably when you called."

"Of course, you know Vic has the funeral plans all spelled out. We haven't made all the arrangements yet, but as soon as they're finalized we'll call you back. Would you be able to do the service on either Friday or Saturday?"

"Either day is fine," Paul said.

"We'll call you tomorrow as soon as we have more details."

"I'll be home all day."

Paul and Susan sat in the kitchen and talked awhile as the full shock sank in. When they returned to bed, his thoughts raced back and forth between the times he had spent with the professor over the past summer to the funeral details themselves. He knew he had a promise to keep with the old man.

Realizing he couldn't sleep, he jumped up and went to the study. There he opened the file drawer of his desk and retrieved the envelope containing Dr. Vickerson's funeral instructions. While Susan had been curious about its contents, Paul had steadfastly refused to open the envelope. He never wanted to face this day, but now it had come.

Paul found himself choked with emotion as he read over the instructions. He still couldn't believe this was happening.

Dr. Vickerson allowed for viewing so that, as he described it, it could 'help everyone face the reality of my death.' The graveside service, according to the professor's wishes, would only involve the family. Following his burial, a memorial service was to be held at the seminary chapel.

The Bradfords drove in on Thursday and stayed at Dr. Vickerson's apartment. Paul went to meet the family. When he knocked, the apartment door opened immediately. A kindly woman stood before him, purse in hand.

"You must be Paul Andrews," she said as she greeted him. "Please come in and have a seat. My husband and I were on the way out the door to the funeral home. I was about to post a note on the door for you to meet us there, but I'm glad you caught us before we left. I have something I need to give you."

An elderly man emerged from the back bedroom. Paul rose to shake hands with him.

"Hello there, Pastor. I'm William Bradford, Dr. Vickerson's brother-in-law. I see you've already met my wife."

"Yes, I have. Nice to meet you both. You'll never know how much your brother means to me, Mrs. Bradford," Paul said, shifting his attention to Dr. Vickerson's sister.

"I would say the feeling was mutual, wouldn't you, Bill?" she answered as she reached in her purse for a tissue.

"Yes, Pastor. Hardly a day went by during his visit that he didn't talk about you. He wondered how your vacation was going—and when he got the postcard..."

"He actually got my card? I can't believe it!" Paul smiled.

"He did, all right. It came just a few days after surgery. He was so tickled when you described your wife's preaching lectures on metaphors and similes! He laughed and said, 'I never intended for him to spend his whole vacation talking about preaching!'"

"That reminds me," Mrs. Bradford said. "Excuse me for one moment, please."

With that she rose from her chair and went back into the bedroom. She returned holding a brown paper bag. As she reached inside the bag, Paul recognized immediately the familiar black leather notebook. He took the fragile volume in his hands and gently fingered the edges of its yellowed and tattered pages.

"If Vic told us once, he told us a dozen times," Mr. Bradford explained, " 'if anything happens to me and I don't come out of the surgery. I want that young man to have my notebook. Make sure he gets that notebook.' He described it to us and told us where we would find it in his desk."

"Yes, he practically drove us crazy," Mrs. Bradford added. "He kept saying, 'If anything happens to me, if anything happens to me.' One day I just snapped back at him and said, 'Will you be quiet, Vic? Quit burying yourself. You'll come out of this surgery just fine. Bill and I will be dead and gone and you'll still be eating those silly cold pizza leftovers for breakfast!' "

On that note her voice cracked, and she began to cry again. Her husband, who seemed almost detached from emotion, picked up the conversation.

"Vic and that pizza!" he laughed. "Do you know, Pastor, he made us go out a few days before his surgery to get that awful pizza? I can't stand the smell of it! Then he brought home the leftovers and you won't believe what he did with them."

"He ate them cold the next morning for breakfast," Paul said quietly.

"How'd you guess?" Mr. Bradford asked with surprise.

"Bill, we'd better get over to the funeral home now. Pastor Andrews, it looks like there will be viewing this evening and Friday. You probably know from Vic's instructions that he only wanted the family at the graveside, with a memorial service at the seminary chapel to follow his burial."

"I know. I read over them after your call the other night. By the way, what about his children?"

"Well, Andy and his wife, Irene, are stationed in the Philippines."

"I'm afraid Dennis is the only one who will be here. He and his wife, Marilyn, will be arriving later this afternoon."

"Such a price our missionaries must pay!" observed Paul.

"Yes, but Vic wouldn't want it any other way. He was so proud of both his children."

"Maybe we should arrange to have the service taped and sent to Andy and Irene," Paul suggested.

"I've already asked the president of the seminary, and he assured me the whole service would be taped on cassette as well as on video."

"Video too!" Paul groaned.

"What's that, Pastor Andrews?"

"Nothing. Video will make a nice memory for them," he said unconvincingly.

"Will we see you at the funeral home tonight?"

"I'll be there. I assume it's the Davidson Home he specified?"

"Yes, the Davidson clan has been operating that home for several generations now. We've known them for many years, but now young David has taken over. His wife, Evelyn, also has her funeral license."

"Dear, I don't think Pastor Andrews is interested in a history of the funeral home," interrupted her husband.

"I'm sorry, you're right," she apologized. "Anyway, the home is just down the street from the seminary."

"I know exactly where it is. We used to joke about certain professors who taught as if they already were . . ." Paul suddenly realized the inappropriateness of the remark. His face reddened as he caught himself and quickly added, "I'll talk to you tonight." The Bradfords either missed what he was about to say or politely ignored it.

As Paul walked back to his car, he felt some guilt about not closing the visit with prayer, but he was afraid he couldn't handle it emotionally. On the way home he decided to apologize to them that evening.

At home Paul went to his study and reread the envelope containing Dr. Vickerson's funeral instructions. Susan entered the room and placed her hands on his shoulders and stood behind him:

"How are the Bradfords doing, Paul?"

"As well as can be expected," he replied somewhat distantly.

"What are you thinking about?"

"I just don't believe what Dr. Vickerson expects me to do," he said. "Read this, Honey. How am I going to do *that* at his memorial service?"

He handed Susan the letter, pointing to the paragraph that upset him. As she read it she slowly slumped to a sitting position on the floor beside his chair.

"I can't believe it either, but you have to do it, Paul. He underlines it and stresses it so strongly that I don't see how you can get out of it. Can you?"

"I guess not. I think I better forewarn his family, though. If I were in their shoes I'd want to know ahead of time what was going to happen." Paul shook his head and laughed weakly. "Dr. Vickerson, Dr. Vickerson! It's just like you to put me up to something like this."

Dr. Vickerson's body was laid out in the familiar old blue suit he wore everywhere. His sister thought of buying a new one for the occasion, then changed her mind. How foolish it would be.

Paul observed that the funeral director had positioned the professor's wooden cane inside the casket, parallel to his body. Visitor after visitor commented about that cane: how it had become such a part of him; how it was only appropriate to include it at his side.

The expression on Dr. Vickerson's face wasn't quite right. His mouth was so fixed that it almost didn't even look like him. That fact was a strange comfort to Paul. It helped him to realize that this was only the body. This servant of the Lord was now present with his Lord.

The notion of preaching in the seminary chapel caught Paul off guard, yet it too was a strange help. Thoughts of preaching before former faculty members and fellow colleagues in the ministry made him slightly nervous, but the tension helped him focus more on the message and less on his own emotional sorrow.

While he was deeply humbled by the honor, at the same time he imagined some people would wonder how and why he was chosen for it. He could think of so many others whom he felt were far more appropriate and qualified than himself.

On Saturday morning Paul and Susan left the boys with their grandparents. Then they went in to meet with the immediate family and make the trip out to Forest Hills Cemetery. He recalled the day the professor so urgently desired to go there to visit his wife's grave—the last time he saw Dr. Vickerson alive.

Before the casket was closed and the small party of people made their way to the cemetery, Paul reached in and removed the cane. Mrs. Bradford gave a silent, approving nod.

Dr. Vickerson's insistence on immediate family created only a slight problem at the grave. The funeral director, his assistant, the two workers who met them at the cemetery, Dr. Vickerson's son, Dennis, and Paul all had to act as pallbearers. Together they transported the casket from the hearse to the grave opening. Paul actually felt honored by the opportunity to carry his professor's body to its final resting place. There he proceeded with a simple, brief committal service in conformity with Dr. Vickerson's instructions.

Afterward, the Bradfords and the Andrews parted company until the memorial service to be held that afternoon. Paul used the time to collect his thoughts and review his notes for the service. He and Susan stopped for a quick lunch, but the growing knot in his stomach warned him to stay away from food until after the service. He ended up ordering a cold cola only.

As they returned to the car, Paul opened the trunk and brought out the little toy saw he had borrowed from James' toolbox.

Carefully he sawed across the middle of Dr. Vickerson's cane. About halfway through he stopped and held it up for examination.

"That should do the trick," he told Susan.

He took the cane and gripped each end of it, centering it over his right knee.

"Don't break it, Paul!" Susan cautioned.

"Don't worry . . . just testing to see if it's ready."

28

A Promise Kept

Paul watched nervously as the chapel began to fill for the service. He recalled how the last and only time he had preached there was as a scared young seminarian who nearly passed out from fright. But now Dr. Vickerson's "Fear Not" conversation came to mind, and he smiled sadly to himself. It had been the professor's final farewell to Paul. "What a farewell!" Paul thought.

Dr. Vickerson's long teaching career and marvelous personality had made him many friends. Paul recognized several professors and former classmates who filed in. He also saw a few other pastors he had come to know over his years in the ministry.

Soon the air on this sunny August afternoon was filled with the fervent singing of Dr. Vickerson's favorite hymns. The inclusion of "Be Thou My Vision" especially choked

Paul up, since this hymn had also been sung at his ordination.

The seminary president and a few faculty members were seated on the platform with Paul. One by one they went to the pulpit to help with various portions of the service. From his perspective Paul could see the young man positioned up in the balcony capturing it all on videotape.

Then came the time to deliver the message. Paul started to approach the pulpit, but after a few steps he turned back. He bent down and reached out a trembling hand for the brown paper bag positioned on the floor beside his seat. He approached the podium for the second time, placing the bag to the side of it. A huge bouquet of flowers served to hide the bag from the congregation's sight.

As he opened his Bible and positioned his notes beside it, Paul caught sight of Susan seated near the front, wearing a warm smile of encouragement. His voice trembled slightly as he read from Psalm 90, but by the time he finished reading and offered a prayer, he began to feel confidence returning, unlike his first attempt at preaching in the chapel.

He began his message. Paul had practiced these introductory words several times when he was alone in his car driving to and from the funeral home during the last two days. But every time he had started, he broke down and wept like a baby. He seldom, if ever, lost control of his emotions in public, but he had never preached on such an occasion as this. Through his tears he kept crying out, "O dear Jesus! How will I ever get through this sermon? Help me, Lord!" This day God's grace flooded his soul as he stood before the congregation.

"I want you to know how God, in His providential care, sent His servant, Dr. William Vickerson, into my life. I first had the privilege of sitting under his teaching over 12 years ago in a seminary homiletics class. He was an excellent and caring teacher, as many of you well know."

Paul noticed many heads nodding in agreement at his last remark.

"The year I graduated, Dr. Vickerson retired. I lost track of him over the next ten years, only to have our paths cross again just a few months ago. If I didn't believe so strongly in God's sovereign rule, I might have thought our meeting was purely accidental. By this time I had lost my initial zeal and enthusiasm for the pulpit and pastorate.

"My ministry was not simply flat, but it was on the brink of disaster. My sermons were as stale and dull as my spirit. I was seriously considering leaving the ministry altogether. If there was any fire left in me the day I ran into Dr. Vickerson, it was that 'dimly smoldering wick' that the Lord Jesus promised He would never snuff out. . . ."

As he continued, Paul's voice grew stronger and stronger. It rang forth with both confidence and joy, yet without minimizing the genuine grief that all were experiencing.

"Then I ran into Dr. Vickerson." he smiled warmly. "I can still see him now, seated across the way inside the library, his cane at his side. Like a mother hen, he took me under his wing and helped to restore my confidence that God had both called me and given me the gifts necessary for this ministry.

You have a great God who loves you more dearly than you love yourself. He called you to this difficult work, but He has also promised to equip you for it and to never leave you or forsake you along the way.

"Dr. Vickerson also helped me sort out my priorities for the pastorate. He showed me in God's Word how I really have just two key responsibilities to my people: prayer and the ministry of the Word.

He taught me new techniques and skills in the preparation and delivery of sermons, while reminding me of
others I had long forgotten—all principles that bring freshness and vitality to preaching.

"You need not take my word for this. Just ask my
congregation. They've noticed the difference, and I am
already witnessing changes in their attitude as a result.
There is a renewed enthusiasm among the people. For all
this and much more I am thankful to the Lord for the rare
privilege of knowing His faithful servant.

"But before I go on, I must admit that one thing bothers
me about this day. Why is it in God's plan that just when
one is so rich and full with the knowledge and experience
of a lifetime of walking in Christ, the Lord calls him home?
There are so many younger preachers who desperately
need what this man was able to give me. Why does the
Lord allow such losses to His dear church?

"Dr. Vickerson's death reminds me of the beautiful
Autumn foliage we will see in October—leaves turning
from shades of green to bright red, yellow, gold, and
brown. Then, as suddenly as they change, they begin to
fall. By early November they are gone, leaving behind the
naked branches. As Robert Frost put it, 'Nothing golden
lasts.' I know our God is perfectly good and wise in all His
ways, but this is still a great mystery to me."

It was only at this point that Paul's voice broke during
the entire message. Again, many in the audience nodded
in agreement. Several men fought back tears, while some
women cried openly.

Paul quickly regained his composure.

"But enough of me. I only say this to honor the man
who has become so dear to us all. I also know that he is
probably pretty angry with me right now for boasting too
much of him," Paul smiled. "He gave me explicit instructions to boast in the Lord and His saving grace. You must
know that before Dr. Vickerson was a preacher or a professor or anything related to his Christian faith and walk,

he was first of all a sinner saved by grace. Although he was raised in a Christian home by two godly parents, William Vickerson will confess to you that he went through a period of rebellion in his late teens and early twenties before returning to the Lord for forgiveness and grace."

Paul went on to emphasize the gospel message, calling on any who had come this day as unbelievers to search their hearts and count the cost of their unbelief. He challenged them with these words:

"What if the situation were reversed today, and this were your funeral and not William Vickerson's? Would you have great peace and assurance that all was well with your soul? Believe me, I have conducted many funerals for those whose families had no such assurance. If you've ever attended such occasions, you have experienced the emptiness and despair that accompanies them. What an awful thing to fall into the hand of the living God with no knowledge of His saving love! My friends, I warn you, if you do not face Christ as Savior and Lord in this life, you must surely face Him as Judge in the life to come!

"The Scripture is very clear in this matter. It says, 'Now is the day of salvation'—not tomorrow, not next week. What if the situation were reversed and this were your funeral? Do you know for sure that if you were to die this very day, you would go to heaven?"

Paul commented on the appropriateness of someone calling on the Lord this day as they gather to remember the ministry of one so dedicated to this very concern. He bowed and prayed in order to give any nonbelievers attending an opportunity then and there to place their trust in the Lord Jesus Christ.

After the prayer he offered comfort to the family and loved ones who would grieve Dr. Vickerson's death most. At one point he faced the videocameras and made some fitting remarks to those overseas in mission work and unable to attend, assuring them that they were right where the Lord and their father wanted them to be during this special day.

Then came time to conclude the message. He turned to 2 Corinthians 4 and began reading in verse 16. By now Paul sensed the power of God's Spirit grip him more strongly than he had ever experienced before.

"The apostle Paul declares to us by the Holy Spirit that the outer man—that is, the body—is decaying. He speaks of the heartaches and trials of life as 'momentary light affliction.' Remember his own afflictions—his thorn in the flesh, his many beatings and persecutions, his imprisonments, the mocking and the shame he underwent for the Lord. He speaks of all that as momentary light affliction!

"That may sound incredible to you, but he means exactly what he says. All this compared to eternity is like nothing! Fleeting! Momentary! Like a little puff of smoke. It's here, then gone!

"And waiting on the other side is what? What's on the other side? I hear some brother back there quoting it for me. Waiting on the other side of death is 'a far more exceeding and eternal weight of glory!' Imagine that! A far more exceeding and eternal weight of glory!" Paul's voice boomed forth with emphasis and victory.

"Take this cane, for example," he said as he reached down into the shopping bag and pulled from it Dr. Vickerson's wooden cane. Lifting it high for all to see, he continued, "William Vickerson leaned on this cane for all these years. Since 1977 he has not spent a day without its assistance. Not a day, that is, until now. Today he needs it no more. And so he has instructed me to do what I'm about to do as a visible sign, to serve as an unforgettable reminder, if you will, that where he is there are no canes, no wheelchairs, no thick glasses, no hearing aids. There are no leg braces or artificial knees. There is no shortage of breath for the asthmatic, nor shortage of strength for one weakened and sapped by disease; no lung cancer, chemotherapy, or radiation treatments. None of that.

"Please be assured, dear friends, that what Dr. Vickerson has instructed me to do here today was not done out of any personal animosity toward God in heaven or toward this inanimate wooden object here on earth. He lived out his latter years grateful for its support and help. There wasn't the slightest hint of anger or bitterness in this man of God.

"But from now on when you think of Dr. William Vickerson, don't imagine for a moment a man weak and crippled, trudging those streets of gold with cane in hand. HE NEEDS THIS CANE NO MORE! PRAISE GOD! HE NEEDS IT NO MORE!"

As Paul said those last words he stepped to the side of the pulpit and seized the cane at each end. From the corner of his eye he caught a glimpse of Dr. Vickerson's sister. Handkerchief in hand, she smiled radiantly through her tears, in anticipation and full knowledge of what was about to happen.

Then holding the cane up high for all to see, he brought it down against his extended knee with a violent force. The clear, crisp snap of the cane splintering in two echoed against the walls and high ceiling of the spacious chapel. Then holding the two halves of the cane high into the air, his face aglow with the Spirit of God, he cried out:

"O DEATH, WHERE IS THY STING? O GRAVE, WHERE IS THY VICTORY?"

Having said it, Paul slowly placed the broken pieces of Dr. Vickerson's cane back in the shopping bag and returned to his seat. After the seminary president pronounced the benediction, the participants in the service left the platform and proceeded up the center aisle leading to the main exit. Susan slipped quietly out of her seat as Paul walked by and accompanied him to the door. She squeezed his hand tightly as they positioned themselves to greet the congregation.

29

Aftermath

The seminary president, who was standing at the door near Paul, shook his hand enthusiastically.

"Young man, your message was excellent. I'm sure Vic is very pleased with what you had to say today—and *how* you said it."

Paul blushed at President Miller's compliment.

"I remember how fond Vic was of Phillip Brooks' definition of preaching: *truth through personality*. I imagine he quoted that to you along the way," Dr. Miller continued.

"Yes, I believe he did," Paul answered. "Why do you mention that?"

"One of Vic's greatest strengths as a preacher was the way his personality so marvelously accompanied the truth of his message. Remember how the apostle Paul told slaves that their lives should *adorn* the doctrine of God?"

"Yes, in the second chapter of Titus."

"Right. Well, I believe very strongly that our personalities, as we preach (as well as when we don't preach), ought to *adorn* the truth rather than *obscure* it. Vic was a master at doing that—both in his lifestyle and in his preaching."

"I know. I've never met anyone quite like Dr. Vickerson," Paul said with admiration.

"I think I've met someone like him," the president responded. "Young man, I can tell you have been his student. Truth came shining through your God-graced personality this afternoon."

"Sir, I don't know what to say," Paul objected.

"Say nothing! It's true. Another man could have preached the very same message. He could have recited it word for word; yet it could have fallen flat. Brooks is right about the importance of the preacher's personality.

"Some of our students and graduates greatly distress me," President Miller continued in a more somber tone. "Their theology is orthodox and their sermons are excellent biblical expositions, yet their effectiveness in ministry is greatly hindered by their determination to divorce personality from preaching. They insist on throwing the truth at their congregations unemotionally, without passion or warmth. They come across as coldhearted and uncaring.

All too often the preacher of the Word strains out the delicious wonders and serves it up with boring dullness, drained of all life!

"At the same time, in private conversations with them, I know they have a great heart for God. Many of them come to me weeping over the lack of visible fruit from their ministry. I wish they could understand that the Scripture teaches them to adorn their preaching with their warmth, their personality. In fact, I feel like making copies of your message today and sending it to them. Maybe it's not too late for them to learn."

While Paul was still reeling from the high compliments of the president, someone grabbed Dr. Miller by the arm and dragged him away from the conversation. A buffet dinner was being hosted by the seminary in Dr. Vickerson's honor, and the president was being consulted by the dining room staff on some last-minute details.

As Paul attempted to offer a parting thank you, he was greeted by his old seminary friend, Barry Longstreet. He was dressed in an expensive business suit, with his tie straight, his hair meticulously in place, and his shoes perfectly shined.

"Barry! It's good to see you!"

"Paul," Barry said as they shook hands, "I, uh, want you to know your message was tremendous."

"Thanks, Barry. That means a lot to me. How are things going with you?"

"Who knows?" Barry said, ignoring the question. "Maybe if I had run into Dr. Vickerson five years ago..."

He stopped in midsentence, unable to complete his words. Then relaxing the grip on Paul's hand, he quickly started out the door.

"Are you staying for the dinner?" Paul asked. "Save me a seat so we can talk."

"No, I have to run. I'm already late for an appointment with one of my clients. He's a big customer. Multimillion dollar business. Can't leave him waiting."

"When would be a good time to get together?" Paul shouted out to him. Barry was now racing down the chapel steps.

"I'll phone you sometime," he called over his shoulder as he continued his hurried pace across the campus.

"Sure, Barry," Paul spoke under his breath. "I'll be waiting to hear from you real soon."

Turning to Susan he asked, "Did you see that watch? Was that a Rolodex?"

"A Rolodex is an office file. You mean a Rolex!" she laughed.

"I know, I know. Just teasing."

"No, it wasn't a Rolex. Barry hasn't quite reached Rolex status yet."

"Still, he looks like he's doing pretty well."

"If God calls you to preach the gospel..." Susan reminded.

"I know—don't stoop along the way to be a king. But sometimes dressing like a king sure looks attractive!"

The next one to greet Paul stood in stark contrast to Barry. His oversized suit was wrinkled and worn; his poorly knotted tie slanted awkwardly to the side; his hair was long and unkempt.

"Reverend," he began, fighting back his tears, "I'm the custodian over at the apartments where Dr. Vickerson lives—lived," he corrected himself. "Today is the first time I've stepped foot inside a church since I was a child. Pray for me, please. I asked Jesus to be my Savior, like you said, but after all these years, would He take an old man like me? After all, look at me, Reverend."

"Oh, yes, most certainly!" Paul responded. "That's the Good News. It's not how young or old we are, who our ancestors are, or how we dress that matters. Nor can we get to heaven by our good works. We get there by trusting in Jesus, who died for our sins on His cross. Do you really mean business about trusting Jesus? If you do, you know your life will be different from now on."

"I mean business, that's for sure. I've watched that man ever since he moved in, wondering what made him so different from everybody else in the apartments. Today you told me what that difference is. Oh, I mean business, Reverend."

"That's wonderful!" Paul answered. "The angels in heaven are rejoicing today. By the way, there's an excellent church just across the corner from the apartments. I know the preacher there teaches the Bible, so why don't you attend tomorrow morning and tell him I sent you? Tell him you prayed here today and trusted Jesus as your Savior. He'll help you understand everything this means."

"I will. I'll start tomorrow." Then the poor custodian looked down at his suit again, and taking the jacket in his hand, asked, "Is it all right to go to church in this, Reverend?"

"That suit will be just fine. I think the worship service starts at 11:00 A.M., but check the bulletin board out front just to make sure."

"I'll do that, and thank you so much."

As the old janitor turned to leave, Susan called out, "Goodbye and God bless you."

"God bless you, ma'am, and you too, Reverend."

Paul continued greeting people. One young boy was fascinated by his cane-breaking trick.

"Do you know karate or something, mister?"

"No, I'm afraid not."

"How'd you break that cane in two, then?"

"That's a secret. Magic!" Paul teased.

"Come on, Paul," Susan prodded. "Tell him how you did it."

"Okay, okay. Here's the big secret. I took a saw and cut about halfway through the middle of the cane so it would easily break in half. When I pulled it out of the shopping bag, I was careful to keep the cut side away from the congregation so they wouldn't see it."

"Oh," was the disappointed reply. Without a further word the boy continued on his way.

"Maybe you should have stuck with the karate idea," Susan laughed. "By the way, whatever made you think of cutting the cane like that?"

"Do you remember the first time I served communion? I tried to break the loaf of bread in two as I said, 'This is my body, broken for you.'"

"I remember!" she laughed. "You pulled and tugged so hard on that bread but you couldn't get it to tear. Your face was red as a beet."

"I finally got it to break apart, but after that I always cut a little slit in the back of the loaf so it would break apart more easily."

"So that's what made you think of sawing the cane."

"Yeah. I know, you just can't get over my brilliance."

After the chapel emptied, Paul and Susan started off toward the cafeteria. Paul was carrying the bag containing the broken cane. He had also placed his Bible and notes in the bag. Susan held his hand as they walked.

"What are you going to do with that cane now? You can't just throw it in the garbage, can you?"

"Excuse me, Pastor Andrews?" a man standing near the cafeteria door interrupted him.

"Yes?"

"May I talk with you alone for a moment?" he asked, glancing toward Susan.

"Paul, why don't I get in line?" she offered. "I'll save you a seat with the Bradfords."

"Be sure to save me some food, too!" he teased.

"Paul? May I call you Paul?" the man asked.

"Sure, and what may I call you?" Paul said as he studied the man before him. He guessed him to be in his mid to late forties. He also surmised he was a minister.

"I'm Charles Fulmer. I'm the pastor of a little Congregational church over on the other side of the city. I've been ordained now for almost 20 years, but in all those years I never heard a sermon like you preached today."

"It was kind of different, to say the least," Paul laughed, uneasy about the compliment.

"No, it was powerful. As you spoke I felt as though I were ushered into the very presence of God!"

"You're kind, but. . ."

"I mean it," he said soberly. "Today as I heard you speak about Dr. Vickerson, and the help he gave you, I kept wishing he were still alive. Like you said in your sermon— you wondered why God calls home His saints when they've grown so mature and ripe in the Lord."

"It's interesting you mention that," Paul responded. "One godly old gentleman came up to me at the door a few moments ago and offered a suggestion as to the why of it."

"Really? What did he say?"

"He said, 'Maybe it happens that way because God in His wisdom knows that if He doesn't call home older believers, you younger ones will never learn to fully stand on your own before the Lord. Each generation has leaders like Moses, who must be taken away by God to make way for the younger Joshuas to rise up and take their places.

'So my advice to you is this: Stand on your own before the Lord. Let go of William Vickerson and hold on to God. Just as you broke that cane before us today, so God has broken and removed the crutch of William Vickerson from you. Learn to lean on God. He's the same yesterday, today, and forever. He can and He will supply all your needs according to His riches in glory!' "

"That's quite a mouthful!" Charles exclaimed. "Ironically, it's that kind of wisdom we younger ones need so much."

"Come to think of it, you're right," Paul replied.

"Maybe this is out of the question," Charles continued, "but I was wondering if you would be willing to share with me some of those principles of preaching you mentioned in your sermon today. My own preaching is so bad. I've gone from church to church to church. Everywhere it's the same: I'm accepted enthusiastically for a year or so, but by my third year the people are tired of me. And they're right— something's terribly wrong with my preaching, and I need to find out what it is.

"The present congregation I serve is ready to fold. I was desperate for work and they were desperate for a pastor; it was the only church willing to call me."

"You won't believe this," Paul answered, "but I promised Dr. Vickerson I would do the very thing you're asking. In fact, I'm going back over my notes right now to prepare a little seminar on preaching. Give me a couple of weeks to catch up from vacation, and we'll get started."

"Really? That sounds wonderful!" Charles' face brightened. "You know, I can't believe how much spiritual pride I have. It has taken me all this time to finally admit that this is my problem. I've accused my people of being unspiritual and dull of hearing. I've pointed the finger at everyone but myself. I've even accused my wife of making too many demands on my time. I can't believe how much I've deceived myself."

"Listen," Paul stopped him. "You don't have to say anything more. I know what you're going through."

After exchanging phone numbers and setting a date for their first meeting, Paul joined Susan at the Bradfords' table.

On the way back to the car Susan asked Paul again what he intended to do with Dr. Vickerson's broken cane.

"Well, I'm afraid Dr. Vickerson has taken care of that little matter also," Paul responded. "You must not have read the end of his instructions or you wouldn't have asked."

"No, you only showed me the part about breaking the cane. So tell me, quick. I'm curious."

"His instructions are to hold on to the broken cane until a cold, snowy winter evening when you, the boys, and I are all home together. I'm to build a fire in our fireplace and get it blazing hot. Then I'm to take the old cane out, show it to the boys, and talk to them about death and the blessing it brings to believers. He wants me to read from Revelation 14:13, where it says, 'Blessed are the dead who die in the Lord.'

"Then after we've had our little service as a family, I'm to give one half of the cane to James and the other half to John and have the boys cast them into the hot flames."

"Then what?"

"Then we're to sit back, watch them burn, and 'bask in the warmth of their heat.' He always told me that after he died the only thing his old cane would be good for was fuel for the fireplace. He wrote that the warmth from the flame might help keep our memories burning strongly till we see him again."

"Leave it to Dr. Vickerson. He sure knows how to go out in style!" Susan laughed.

The parking lot was nearly empty now. The sun was starting to sink behind the trees to the west of the campus. A soft summer evening breeze began to blow, refreshing Paul's face after the long, hot, and emotionally draining day. Inside he felt sadness mixed with unspeakable joy.

At the car he paused long enough to open the door and toss the bag onto the back seat. Then he took Susan's hand and the two walked on. She looked at him with slight surprise when they passed their car and started out of the parking lot.

Out onto the sidewalk in front of the seminary they headed for Elmhurst Street, where they stopped briefly across from Dr. Vickerson's old house.

"Just think," Paul said as he caught glimpse of a stranger standing in the front living room by the picture window. "As much as Dr. Vickerson and his wife loved their home, they are in a far greater place—that place Christ prepared for them before the foundation of the world."

As they walked on they passed their old seminary apartment and began to reminisce about how much had changed in ten years. James and John had come along, and with them old Snooper and three goldfish. Thinking of the two boys startled Susan; it had been early in the morning since they dropped the boys off.

"We better start back, Paul. It's been a long day."

"What's the hurry?" he asked with a smile.

"For one thing, it's not fair to leave the boys so long at their grandparents. And why do you have that sly look on your face, Paul Andrews?"

"Listen," he grinned. "I made other arrangements for tonight. The boys are staying with grandma and grandpa. You and I are spending this evening together, alone, at our favorite hotel."

"I don't understand."

"Well, do I have to preach tomorrow?"

"No, but . . ."

"And isn't it rare for me to get a weekend off, and rarer still for us to ever be alone, given the presence of our two sons?"

"Yes, but . . ."

"And didn't we spend the first night of our honeymoon at the downtown Sheraton?"

"Yes, but what about clothing and . . ."

"Well, there just happens to be a small suitcase in our trunk. Besides, what's to stop us from visiting one of your favorite shops over at town square if you're not satisfied with what I packed? The reservations are made. The kids are taken care of. We have all evening and all day tomorrow to be together."

Susan embraced Paul tightly and smiled.

"You know, I never had a chance to tell you how well you did in chapel today. Your message was outstanding."

"Sometimes when people say they give God all the glory, it sounds so trite, like they don't even think about what they're saying. But tonight I can say it and really mean it. To God be the glory! I never would have made it without His grace."

As darkness fell over the city, the sweet summer breeze refused to die as it gently brushed their faces. Deep inside Paul's heart another breeze had also been blowing as of late, one that brought new freshness and zeal to his high calling. He knew now that he could never turn away from that calling, not even if someone offered him a kingdom in its place. For the first time in many years he looked forward to the new fall season with excitement.

30

A Seminar on Fresh Preaching

Paul Andrews kept his promise to Dr. Vickerson and to Charles Fulmer: He met with Charles every Monday morning between September and Christmas. Together they went over the principles of preaching taken from Paul's notes and study assignments.

They also agreed to preach on the same passages each week so they could benefit even more from their time together. Each came with a basic outline of his sermon a week in advance, so they could share ideas and insights and discuss problems they were having.

Paul arranged his seminar notes in four parts. First came the high priority of preaching. The second section covered the study of the text, the discovery of its purpose, and the shaping of the sermon outline. Third came the application of various principles to the sermon body to develop the message with freshness and power. Last, he included a section on long-term planning for freshness in preaching.

Repeating the whole process helped Paul to sharpen his own grasp on the principles and his skill in applying them to his preaching. Weekly feedback from his congregation grew more positive all the time. For the first time in several years the Sunday morning attendance was picking up.

Remember how the apostle Paul told slaves that their lives should **adorn** *the doctrine of God? Our personalities, as we preach, ought to* **adorn** *the truth rather than* **obscure** *it.*

For Charles the process was far more difficult. He found it hard to break habits formed from 20 years of poor preaching. Dr. Miller's remarks about preaching as "truth through personality" were almost prophetic. This was precisely Charles' greatest problem, as Paul discovered upon listening to one of his sermon tapes. The content of the message was solid and sound, but the delivery was impersonal and cold.

When Paul questioned him on his philosophy of preaching as it related to personality, he was shocked at Charles' response. Evidentally the pastor who was instrumental in Charles' call to the ministry had instructed him, among other things, to "never look the congregation in the eye. Always look over their heads to an imaginary spot at the back of the sanctuary. That way you won't make anyone think you are preaching specifically to him."

He also had urged Charles to avoid personal illustrations and any intrusion of personal emotions into the message. The result of his advice and example had been 20 long years of dry sermons, delivered without emotion or eye contact. As President Miller had observed, truth was *obscured* rather than *adorned* by personality.

Gradually, though, Charles began to catch fire. By early December Paul noticed a marked improvement in his attitude as well as his preaching. His personality was beginning to break through into his preaching, with positive results.

In the meantime Charles' little congregation, although beginning to notice improvement, still hung by a thread to their existence. Being such a small church added special problems to his challenge as their pastor.

As Christmas approached, however, a new family from the neighborhood began to attend. Having never heard Charles' preaching before, they could only compare it with their former pastor. Their enthusiastic response was the long-awaited encouragement he needed. From that time forward his excitement and drive for excellence began to accelerate.

The crowning achievement of Paul's work with him came on Christmas Eve. A young man attending the candlelight service with his girlfriend responded to the challenge that Charles gave to receive the gift of eternal life, the true gift of Christmas offered to us in God's Son. After the service the young man greeted Charles at the door with the news that he had trusted Christ that night. Charles was so excited that he called Paul on Christmas morning with the news.

Charles made an important observation near the end of their seminar together. When he reflected on his earlier impatience to see immediate results, he realized that three or four months was such a short time to see such good progress when compared to the 20 years of ministry that went before it.

That realization caused both hope and sadness: hope for future improvement, but sadness over 20 impoverished years. Charles chastised himself for waiting so long to find help, and he expressed a strong desire to find other pastors who might be in similar straits, needing similar help and encouragement. It seems so hard for preachers to admit when they are poor at preaching, since it is so central to their calling.

At the end of the seminar Paul and Charles were reluctant to stop meeting together. Having forged a friendship they did not want to see broken, they continued their weekly meetings to discuss coming sermons and to evaluate the previous week's efforts. Keeping two weeks ahead in their exegesis of the text helped them keep their messages sharp and well-prepared.

Charles soon realized, however, how easy it was to forget to use all the principles of freshness he had learned from Paul, so he prepared a one-page checklist of the key ideas he had learned. He reduced the checklist on a copier to a size that fit just inside the back cover of his Bible, so he could refer to it as a final review before concluding that Sunday's sermon was fully prepared.

He posted a copy near his desk and gave his checklist to Paul to use. It proved so valuable to Paul he attached it to his seminar notes as a summary of Dr. Vickerson's principles of preaching with freshness.

Preaching-with-Freshness Checklist

Initial Sermon Preparation

1. Is series planned in advance?
2. Start early: exegesis, not eisegesis.
3. Discover Holy Spirit's purpose.
4. Make His purpose your sermon's purpose.
5. Attack material early, often, with intervals of rest between study.
6. Shape sermon's purpose or *destination* into an *aphorism*.
7. Reword old clichés, if necessary.

Preparing the Sermon Outline

1. Choose best *vehicle* to drive sermon to its *destination*.
2. Vary the vehicle weekly to arouse audience curiosity.
3. Choices of vehicles to use:
     Expository, verse-by-verse
     Topical sermon
     Narrative/biographical
          (first-person account as one form of narrative)
     Antithetical sermon
     Procedural sermon
     Persuasive sermon
     Repetition sermon
4. Keep outline simple and easy to follow, logical.

Improve Upon Sermon Body

1. Strong *introduction*, to the point.
2. Use *surprise power* where possible.

3. Create *internal dialogue* through: questions, puzzles, riddles, and mind-teasers.

4. *Three R's* of preaching: reminding, repeating, reiterating.

5. *Fitting illustrations* (finish outline early enough to find them).

6. "Midweek" prayer meeting: Seek God's guidance for application to audience.

7. Vocabulary: *Sense appeal, not snob appeal*—"word pictures."

8. Use "nondictionary sounds" if needed.

9. Use *Metaphors and similies*.

10. *Second person* ("you") preaching.

11. *Humor* should be natural, not canned. Use *hyperbole* and *exaggeration*.

12. *Strong conclusion* to drive home point.

13. Are you filled with *reservoir power*? Fitting scholarship, full of prayer, Holy Spirit *unction*, full of the Word?

14. Have you *polled* congregation on subject?

Keys to Long-Term Freshness

1. *WIDE RANGE OF READING:*
   Use of the "sixfold path" by reading in six different areas at one time (novels, historical, biography, diary/journal, poetry, and some "hot" interest topic).

2. *GATHERING ILLUSTRATIONS:*
   One day/month to gather, file, and review. Collect illustrations from newspaper articles, periodicals in local library, "sixfold" reading books, and personal daily events. Try creating your own. Have shut-in members read books you don't have time to read, scanning for illustrations they think you might use.

3. *PRACTICE SELF-EVALUATION:*
   Listen to your tapes, if possible; have yourself videotaped; ask for help from spouse or fellow pastor; critique

voice, timing of message, your "personality" in the message.

4. *STUDY GREAT PREACHERS' SERMONS*
   Books of sermons by past masters of preaching; tapes/videos of recent ones; radio/television of present. Learn to use their strengths in your preaching, yet without aping them.

5. Read one good book on preaching per year.

6. Attend refreshers, seminars, D.Mins.

7. Plan your sermon series a year in advance.

8. Carry a copy of the series' schedule inside your Bible cover for a reminder.

9. Let "iron sharpen iron" through discussions with fellow preachers.

A condensed one-page version of this checklist
is included to provide easy access to this information.

PREACHING-WITH-FRESHNESS CHECKLIST

Initial Sermon Preparation

1. Is series planned in advance?
2. Start early: exegesis, not eisegesis.
3. Discover Holy Spirit's purpose.
4. Make His purpose your sermon's purpose.
5. Attack material early, often, with intervals of rest between study.
6. Shape sermon's purpose or *destination* into an *aphorism*.
7. Reword old clichés, if necessary.

Preparing the Sermon Outline

1. Choose best *vehicle* to drive sermon to its *destination*.
2. Vary the vehicle weekly to arouse audience curiosity.
3. Choices of vehicles to use: Expository, verse-by-verse
   Topical sermon
   Narrative/biographical
   (first-person account as one form of narrative)
   Antithetical sermon
   Procedural sermon
   Persuasive sermon
   Repetition sermon
4. Keep outline simple and easy to follow, logical.

Improve Upon Sermon Body

1. Strong *introduction*, to the point.
2. Use *surprise power* where possible.
3. Create *internal dialogue* through: questions, puzzles, riddles, and mind-teasers.
4. *Three R's* of preaching: reminding, repeating, reiterating.
5. *Fitting illustrations* (finish outline early enough to find them).
6. "Midweek" prayer meeting: Seek God's guidance for application to audience.
7. Vocabulary: *Sense appeal, not snob appeal*—"word pictures."
8. Use "nondictionary sounds" if needed.
9. Use *Metaphors and similies.*
10. *Second person* ("you") preaching.
11. *Humor* should be natural, not canned. Use *hyperbole* and *exaggeration*.
12. *Strong conclusion* to drive home point.
13. Are you filled with *reservoir power*? Fitting scholarship, full of prayer, Holy Spirit *unction*, full of the Word?
14. Have you *polled* congregation on subject?

Keys to Long-Term Freshness

1. *WIDE RANGE OF READING:*
   Use of the "sixfold path" by reading in six different areas at one time (novels, historical, biography, diary/journal, poetry, and some "hot" interest topic).

2. *GATHERING ILLUSTRATIONS:*
   One day/month to gather, file, and review. Collect illustrations from newspaper articles, periodicals in local library, "sixfold" reading books, and personal daily events. Try creating your own. Have shut-in members read books you don't have time to read, scanning for illustrations they think you might use.

3. *PRACTICE SELF-EVALUATION:*
   Listen to your tapes, if possible; have yourself video-taped; ask for help from spouse or fellow pastor; critique voice, timing of message, your "personality" in the message.

4. *STUDY GREAT PREACHERS' SERMONS*
   Books of sermons by past masters of preaching; tapes/videos of recent ones; radio/television of present. Learn to use their strengths in your preaching, yet without aping them.

5. Read one good book on preaching per year.

6. Attend refreshers, seminars, D.Mins.

7. Plan your sermon series a year in advance.

8. Carry a copy of the series' schedule inside your Bible cover for a reminder.

9. Let "iron sharpen iron" through discussions with fellow preachers.

Paul's Seminar on
Preaching with Freshness and Power

I. THE PRIORITY OF PREACHING

A. Acts 6:1-4 and Ephesians 4:8-12.
1. Make prayer and ministry of the Word your high calling.
2. Beecher's *Preaching: The Preacher's Whole Business*.
3. Are the streams flowing toward or away from your pulpit?
4. Filter all activities through Acts 6:1-4.
5. Are you busy at "church work" or your Father's business?

B. Start to rearrange your life by the priorities in Acts 6:1-4.
1. Do a time study to evaluate your present situation.
2. Approach your Church Board with results of study.
3. Plan with Board ways to restructure your time accordingly.
4. Plan with Board ways to communicate changes to congregation.

C. See the importance of starting early.
1. Plan the sermon series in advance.
2. Begin sermon preparations early in the week.
3. Use the attack-rest-attack-rest approach.

D. Avoid the trap of destructive and wasteful pressures.

E. Learn to harness creative energies instead.

II. PREPARING THE SERMON OUTLINE

A. Use early exegesis to avoid late eisegesis.
1. Discover the Holy Spirit's purpose for inspiring the text.

2. Match your sermon's purpose with the Holy Spirit's purpose.
3. Your purpose then becomes the sermon's goal or *destination*.
4. Shape the purpose statement into an *aphorism*.
   Aphorism: A short, pointed sentence expressing a truth or a precept: maxim, adage.
   a. Example: Matthew 6:21: Where your treasure is . . .
      Example: Matthew 6:24: You cannot serve God and mammon.
   b. Reword worn-out clichés to make new aphorisms.

B. Next choose the best *vehicle* to reach that *destination*.
1. Vary your outlines from week to week to arouse curiosity of congregation *before* you even begin the sermon.
2. Outlines should be simple, each point helping you recall the next point, flowing naturally and logically.
3. Don't tell congregation how many points your sermon has! They'll start counting. Avoid things like "My final point is . . ."

Various sermon outlines and approaches to choose from:

1. *Expository* sermon: Scripture itself has great variety.
2. *Topical* sermon: Don't twist passages to fit your topic.
3. *Narrative* and/or *Biographical* sermon.
   a. Does it sacrifice substance? You may communicate less truths, but in a more memorable fashion (parables).
   b. Biographical: People listen closely as they identify with the personalities of Bible characters.
   c. Easier for preacher to remember sermon, less notes, more eye contact with congregation.
   d. If your sermon outline is so complicated that you must follow it carefully, how will your people remember it?
4. *Antithetical* sermon.
   a. Common in Scripture: light vs. darkness; God vs. mammon; sand vs. solid rock; rich man vs. poor Lazarus; etc.

   b. Contrasts are easy for congregation to follow.

   c. Use body language to indicate two opposing points.

   d. Even though congregation won't remember every point of contrast, they will remember the main point.

5. *Persuasive* sermon.

   a. Every sermon persuades, but this refers to kind of preaching Paul did in Acts: "reasoning and arguing."

   b. Doctrinal issues like trinity, baptism, tongues.

   c. Touchy ethical issues like abortion, medical ethics.

   d. Important steps in preparing for such a message:

     1) Anticipate opponents' attitudes and objections.

     2) Be kind and nondefensive, secure in position.

     3) Show genuine appreciation for opponents' concerns.

     4) Thank them for challenge to carefully examine truth.

     5) Admit abuses of your position, if necessary.

     6) Present solid scriptural and logical evidences.

     7) Arrange argument carefully, climax at end.

     8) Bathe matter in prayer.

     9) Don't neglect dialogue with opponents *before* as well as after sermon. Don't hide behind the pulpit!

     10) Speak boldly and unapologetically for truth.

6. *Procedural* sermon: Practical "how to" message.

   a. Avoid trite, superficial treatment of problems.

   b. Dig deep, spend time in study, prayer, dialogue with others dealing with the issue.

   c. One sermon you can number the points. Example: "Four Steps Toward Experiencing Forgiveness"; "The Steps of Church Discipline."

7. *Repetition* sermon: Good repetition involves three elements.

   a. A theme worth repeating. Example: "It's Friday, But Sunday's Coming!"

   b. Strong supporting evidences and materials sandwiched between each repetition of the theme.

c. Strategic ordering of those materials so that each builds on what went before, leading to a powerful and dramatic conclusion.

III. EMPLOYING TECHNIQUES OF FRESHNESS ON THE SERMON BODY

A. Use *surprise power*: Often we overlook the surprising nature of God's Truth as it is found in the text.

Example: The other "little boats" on the lake when Jesus called the storm.

Example: Paul's quoting a pagan philosopher who calls Cretans liars, evil beasts, and lazy gluttons—yet expecting Titus to find godly men on Crete to serve as elders!

B. Create *internal dialogue* in the minds of the listeners by—

1. Asking questions (not to be answered aloud, but internally in the minds of the hearers). 237 questions on lips of Jesus in the Gospel accounts, not asked for His information but to prod others to think.

2. Offering puzzles, riddles, and mind-teasers to be solved (example: How can Christ be both David's Son and his Lord? See Mark 12:35-37).

C. Use the *three R's of preaching*:

1. *Reminding*: Most preaching is reminding from week to week.

(Key is to remind in refreshing terms and ways.)

2. *Repetition*: See section II. B. 7. above.

3. *Reiteration*:Repeating an idea in other words:

a. Usually within the same thought or paragraph.

b. Preaching is for the ear to hear, not the eye to read.

c. Reiteration allows idea to sink in, aids memory.

Example: Hebrew poetry in couplet form (Isaiah 53).

Example: Sermon on the Mt. (God and mammon).

Example: Illustrations also reiterate.

D. Turn on the light of *illustrations*.

Definition: "To shed light on, to make bright, make clear."

1. Gather them: Always keep illustration notebook nearby. "Illustrations, like babies, have a habit of being born at awkward times."
2. Where to find them—magazines, books, newspapers, objects and incidents in everyday life, preaching publications.
3. File and save them.
   Learn from the ants—Proverbs 6:6-8.
   Learn from Joseph—save during "fat" times for "lean" times.
   a. Choose a system you'll use—3x5 cards, file folders, three-ring binders, computer listing, etc.
   b. Review them periodically as reminder of what you have.
   c. Additional hint: Keep a "Best Illustrations" file for use on outside speaking occasions.
4. Tailor them to fit the sermon.
   Example: If headlights aren't adjusted, they may illuminate the air instead of the road.
   a. Don't force latest illustration you heard into next week's sermon if it doesn't fit.
   b. Feel free to edit extraneous details to better fit sermon (without changing truth of illustration).
5. Dangers to avoid.
   a. Illustrations that send congregation off on tangents.
   b. Illustrations that overpower sermon's message.
   Example: The joke that doesn't quite fit.
   Example: A story so powerful that it reshapes whole message.
6. Don't try to fit in illustrations too soon.
   a. Wait until outline of sermon is clear.
   b. Don't bend sermon to fit illustration; choose illustration that best fits sermon.
7. Don't wait too late to find illustrations.
   a. Gather and file them year-round.
   b. Finish sermon outline early enough to find fitting illustrations (Saturday night is usually too late).

E. Improve your *preaching vocabulary*.

   1. Aim at staying within the vocabulary of your members.

     (Average "common" vocabulary = 5000 words.)

   2. Strive for Pascal's "eloquence that despises eloquence."

   3. Use *sense appeal*, not *snob appeal*.

     a. Avoid words that impress others with your knowledge.

     b. Use words that impress others with the truth: five senses—touch, taste, smell, sight, hearing.

   4. Exercises to improve preaching vocabulary:

     a. Watch for fresh words and phrases in commentaries.

     b. Look for them in outside readings.

     c. Study/underline sense-appeal words in pocket dictionary.

     d. Write and rewrite key portions of sermon accordingly. *Avoid danger of poor eye contact: Be well prepared so you can rely on as few notes as possible in the pulpit!*

     e. Learn to create "word pictures" in listeners' minds.

F. Use *non-dictionary sounds* to better communicate.

   Example: Imitate Jonah snoring in the boat, storm raging above.

G. Use more —second-person preaching.

   Example: Waitress asks "Are *we* ready to order yet?"

   Example: "Are we walking in Christ?" to "Are you walking in Christ?" Notice the important change in focus and power this brings to your preaching.

H. Learn to better use the power of *metaphors and similes*. Aristotle quote: Best by far to be "master of the metaphor."

   1. Definitions and differences: Similes add "like" or "as."

   2. By doing so, they weaken the tension of the analogy.

I. Use the power of *humor*: its place and importance.

   1. Natural humor versus "canned" jokes.

   2. The use of *exaggeration* and *hyperbole*.

   3. Benefits of good humor:

     a. Rests the congregation after intense thinking.

b. Relieves tensions/opens hearts to hear message.

c. Holds the congregation's attention, keeps sermon moving.

d. Makes point in memorable fashion.
Example: Straining out the gnat and swallowing the camel.

IV. KEYS TO LONG-TERM FRESHNESS AND POWER

A. Enter the pulpit with full *reservoir power.*

1. Is your sermon full of scholarship?

   a. Not for sake of impressing others with your knowledge.

   b. Nor losing them by being "too deep."

   c. Nor bathing them in Bible trivial.

   d. But giving them key insights into the customs and times.

   e. Insights that focus their eyes on Christ, not you.

2. Are you full of the Word of God?
Each week read through whole book or large portion of Bible (in addition to the study of Sunday's text).

3. Are you full of prayer?
Fervent prayer shows your reliance on God, not self.

   a. Hold a personal "mid-week prayer meeting" over your sermon's direction and congregation's needs from it.

   b. Remember to pray for fellow pastors' ministries.
This is a good test of your sincerity for God's glory.

4. Are you full of God's Spirit?

   a. *Unction* is hard to define.

   b. But people know whether you have it or not.

B. Practice ongoing *self-evaluation.*

1. Listen to your own sermon tapes.

   a. Watch for strong *introductions* and *conclusions.*

      1) Use the introduction to clue congregation as to the application of the sermon to their lives. Whet their appetites early!

      2) Make sure the conclusion hits the mark promised in the introduction.

      3) Be brave enough to leave unnecessary data from your preparation in the study.

      4) Include only enough exegesis to demonstrate the biblical authority undergirding your applications.

    b. Remove annoying speech mannerisms.

2. Use videotapes if available, or help of spouse or others.

    a. Watch for annoying body movements, quirks.

    b. Are body gestures large enough to communicate?

    c. Do gestures match content of sermon?

    d. Do facial expressions match content of sermon? Example: Do you frown when talking of heaven, smile for hell?

3. Voice—inflection, enthusiasm.

    a. Watch for sagging enthusiasm as sermon goes on.

    b. Is your inflection as strong as you imagined?

    c. Avoid "preacher tone"; use more conversational style.

    d. Does your voice drop too low at end of sentences?

    e. Enough good variety to tone and intensity of your voice?

4. Timing: Work on removing "drag" times in messages.

    a. Don't belabor a point (sign of poor preparation).

    b. Add appropriate humor, illustrations, voice shifts, etc.

    c. Be prepared well enough to maintain good eye contact.

    d. Learn to "read" audience and adjust sermon accordingly.

5. Is your sermon clear and descriptive in expression?

6. Is it easy to follow your sermon's logic and outline?

7. Does your personality *adorn* the truth or *obscure* it?

    a. Are you too impersonal? Add warmth, personal illustrations. Include the whole range of human emotions.

    b. Are you too self-centered? Too many personal illustrations, too much bragging, self-exalting?

    c. What is the underlying tone of your personality? Are you constantly angry? Self-righteous in your pronouncements? Too bland, too safe, too wishy-washy? Or does a well-balanced, grace-filled personality come through with the message?

  8. Does your sermon reflect the pulse of your congregation and community?

    a. Have you informally polled members and the "man on the street" on the sermon topic? (Don't miss this witnessing opportunity!)

    b. Is there a freshness that comes from being on "the cutting edge" concerning the topic at hand?

    c. Or must you dig into the past to find an occasion when you talked to someone about the topic?

C. Practice extensive reading in fields other than ministry.

  1. Sixfold path.

    a. Read from six different books at a time instead of only one.

    b. Choose from five categories, such as: novels, historical books, biographies, diaries and journals, and poetry.

    c. Choose one from a "hot" topic or personal concern.

  2. Spend a day each month in library periodical room.

  3. Use seminary library if available.

  4. Continually gather, file, and review illustrations.

D. Practice long-term sermon planning.

  1. Evaluate the congregation's weakness and long-term needs.

  2. Use summer slowdown to plan entire sermon year.

  3. Keep sermon schedule inside Bible cover as a reminder.

E. *Sermon analysis*: Learn from the masters of preaching.

  1. Study sermons of preaching greats.

  2. Listen to sermon tapes of great preachers.

  3. Study videos or televised sermons of great preachers.

  4. Learn especially from their strengths.

  5. Keep a notebook of strengths.

F. *Refreshers*: Study and review preaching techniques.

  1. Periodically review seminar notes as reminder.

2. Read one good book on preaching each year.
3. Interact with colleagues on preaching; let "iron sharpen iron."
4. Take advantage of seminars and refresher courses offered.

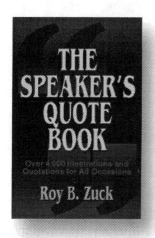

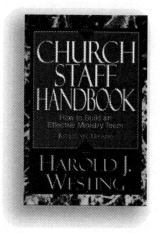